I0619887

# ANCIENT WISDOM
# FOR MODERN TIMES

*Biblical Foundations for Life in a*

*World That Has Lost Its Way*

**Reuben J Rose**

COPYRIGHT PAGE © 2023

All Bible quotes from the New King James Version (NKJV) of the Bible unless otherwise specified. With some of the quotes, I have added emphases that were not in the original.

All rights reserved. No part of this publication may be reproduced, distributed or transmitted in any form or by any means, including photo-copying, recording, or other electronic or mechanical methods, without the prior written permission of the publisher, except in the case of brief quotations embodied in critical reviews and certain other non-com-mercial uses permitted by copyright law.

Although the author and publisher have made every effort to ensure that the information in this book was correct at press time, the author and publisher do not assume and hereby disclaim any liability to any party for any loss, damage, or disruption caused by errors or omissions, whether such errors or omissions result from negligence, accident, or any other cause.

Adherence to all applicable laws and regulations, including interna-tional, federal, state and local governing professional licensing, business practices, advertising, and all other aspects of doing business in the US, Canada or any other jurisdiction, is the sole responsibility of the reader and consumer.

Neither the author nor the publisher assumes any responsibility or liability whatsoever on behalf of the consumer or reader of this material. Any perceived slight of any individual or organization is purely unintentional.

The resources in this book are provided for informational purposes only. They should not be used to replace the specialized training and profes-sional judgment of a health care or mental health care professional.

Neither the author nor the publisher can be held responsible for the use of the information provided within this book. Please always consult a trained professional before making any decision regarding the treatment of yourself or others.

For more information, email reuben@bolocorose.com or visit https://www.inancientpaths.com/free-workbook.php

ISBN: 979-8-89109-114-6 -paperback

ISBN: 979-8-89109-115-3 - ebook

ISBN? 979-885780-528-2 - hardcover

*To my wife Kate, who has helped me discover and understand the ancient paths that lead to life.*

Thank you for buying *Ancient Wisdom for Modern Times*. For more information, please visit my book website: https://www.inancientpaths.com/free-workbook.php

There is a short video that gives more information about the book's background. You can also download a free workbook that can be used individually and for groups. The workbook is in a pdf format and has a series of questions, associated with each chapter, that aim to help book readers explore ideas about wisdom in their own lives.

# Table of Contents

# FOREWORD

*Ancient Wisdom for Modern Times*. Oh, how I could have used some of that in my earlier days and even more so now.

As a child growing up in the rural Midwest, I didn't give much thought about wisdom at all. I simply did "my thing" and had a fool's confidence that everything would just work out the way that it was supposed to in the grand scheme of life. Later, in my mid-twenties, I had a personal encounter with Jesus that changed my life forever. However, my flippant attitude toward wisdom continued to develop into an imperceivable arrogance. I now assumed that by virtue of knowing the LORD personally, I somehow embodied an innate "wisdom" of my own that I could simply draw upon at will whenever I needed to make decisions. Well, as an older man in my fifties, I can confidently say that my history of failed businesses, divorce, and reoccurring cycles of being overwhelmed have betrayed my past approach to understanding, obtaining, and applying divine wisdom in my life. Today, I can humbly agree with King Solomon that wisdom is not to be assumed or, even worse, ignored, but rather it is to be diligently sought after, and obtaining her is far more precious than all the treasures that the world has to offer (Proverbs 8:11).

Maybe looking back over your life, you find yourself in a similar position, or perhaps you've still never given much thought to what wisdom really is, understanding that there's a difference between the wisdom of the world and the wisdom of God or how you even begin to seek, obtain, and apply divine wisdom in your life. Well, I've got good news for you! If you're holding this book in your hands, the LORD is placing wisdom at your doorstep, and she's crying out for you to listen. Maybe you've prayed for wisdom, and this is His answer. Perhaps you *will* pray for wisdom, and the LORD is answering you even before you ask! You know He can do that. Either way, I don't believe in chance or luck. So, if you're reading this, just know that your Father, the One who loves you and has a great plan for your life, is giving you a divine opportunity to hear and receive some of His ancient wisdom.

Over the past twenty-five years, I've had the privilege of teaching, training, ministering, and meeting some of the most excellent people in the world. Truly, their hearts, lives, and love for the LORD have provoked me unto greater vision, intimacy with God, and pursuit of His Kingdom than I could have ever imagined. Reuben Rose is one of these rare saints, and yet in my life, he's truly in a class of his own. I met Reuben in Kansas City, Missouri, in 2012 at a training I was leading on the end-time prayer movement, and after spending much time with him, both in America and his beautiful home country of Australia, I can unreservedly say that he is the "real deal." Beyond his age, credentials, and accomplishments (which are many), it is Reuben's desire to love extravagantly and keep growing, his commitment to do all things with excellence and learn from his mistakes, and his ability to be vulnerable, see beyond the obvious and ask people the right questions that uniquely qualifies him as a father who has found some of God's hidden riches to share.

I've heard it said, *"It's not how you start the race that counts but how you finish,"* and that couldn't be more true when speaking of your life and the course you've set for the journey. So regardless of how you began this race or where you find yourself right now, I pray that the precious nuggets of wisdom that Reuben has gained over a lifetime of experience be granted to you, and may the LORD Jesus Christ empower you through His divine wisdom to finish your race strong, in order to hear the words, *"Well done, good and faithful servant"* (Matthew 25:21).

Corey Stark

**Executive Director at Ignite The Nations**

www.ignitethenations111.org

# INTRODUCTION

We live in a time where information is at everyone's fingertips. Internet searches can turn up millions of "hits" in seconds. With the increase in the availability of information, it is hard to find relevant and appropriate knowledge, and now there is debate about what is "truth." It is an age-old question that Pontius Pilate asked, apparently rhetorically, to Jesus around 2,000 years ago (John 18:38). Today, with the awareness of "fake news," finding the truth is an ongoing challenge. Additionally, post-modernism declares that there is no such thing as truth but rather "my truth" or "your truth."

How do we respond to this problem of information overload and bias? How do we find the truth? Well—there was a man, Jesus, who proclaimed something extraordinary in Galilee 20 centuries ago that has stood the test of time. In response to His disciples asking, "How can we know the way?" Jesus said, "I am the way, **the truth** and the life." (John 14:6). Remarkably, we find in this statement that the truth is a person, and Jesus says that in knowing Him, we can see the truth. By corollary, if we don't know Jesus, we will stumble around trying to find truth and be blown with the winds of current thinking and whatever direction they take. I believe the best guide in our modern quest for truth is the ancient writings of the Old Testament and the New Testament, brought together in the sixty-six books of the Bible.

It is interesting to reflect on the rise of the United States as a world power and the fact that the Bible was one of the critical documents for children in U.S. schools to read until the early 1950s. Constitutional legal challenges to freedom of religion resulted in the Bible being taken out of public schools and, therefore, the Truth disappearing. The U.S. Founding Fathers understood the importance of the ancient paths and revered the Bible. John Adams famously stated, "Our Constitution was made only for a moral and religious people. It is wholly inadequate to the government of any other."[1] This was the view of the founders of the U.S. Constitution,[2] where those who wrote the Constitution understood that "God's moral inclinations are intrinsically woven into the design and nature of creation."[2] These verities, well accepted by our forebears, are the elements of wisdom that, when learned, allow us to prosper individually and together as a society.

Thus, surprisingly, the key to finding our way in increasingly difficult modern times is returning to ancient truths outlined in the Bible. As Jesus sent out the 70 disciples, it is interesting that his advice was to be "as wise as serpents and innocent as doves" (Matthew 10:16). What does this mean? It's hard to know precisely because we need the wisdom to understand! However, at the very least, Jesus was warning his followers to be alert, exercise discernment, and be prudent in their decisions and interactions with the people who came across their paths.

**So what is wisdom?** The **Cambridge Dictionary defines wisdom as** *"the ability to use your knowledge and experience to make good*

---

1  https://constitutionallaw.regent.edu/preserving-a-constitution-de-signed-for-a-moral-and-religious-people/

2  https://www.theologyfortherestofus.com/natural-law-definition-history-and-examples

*decisions and judgments."*[3] Merriam-Webster,[4] acknowledging the complexity of ideas about wisdom, provides several definitions:

*"Ability to discern inner qualities and relationships, good sense, generally accepted belief, accumulated philosophical or scientific learning; a wise attitude, belief, or course of action; the teachings of ancient wise men."* The definition includes the following synonyms for wisdom: *discernment, insight, perception, and sagacity.* The most often-used word for the opposite of wisdom is foolishness. According to this definition, wisdom is an inner quality linked in some way to decision-making or "a course of action" and correlates to good decisions.

Even amongst secular scholars, King Solomon, who lived around 1,000 years before Jesus' birth, is recognized as the wisest man who ever lived. It is significant that when God asked Solomon in a dream at Gibeon, "What shall I give you" Solomon chose what could broadly be described as wisdom (1 Kings 3:9). The NKJV translates this as an "understanding heart," but the Hebrew word is שׁמַע (*šâmaʻ*), which in English conveys the sense of "to hear intelligently and with obedience." Solomon's request for an understanding heart was so that he might discern between good and evil (1 Kings 3:9). God was pleased with King Solomon's request and said He would give Solomon a "wise and discerning mind." Wisdom then, as outlined in the Bible, is a gift of God, and 1,000 years later, in the New Testament, this is confirmed by James, Jesus' half-brother, who was the church leader in Jerusalem. James says, "If any of you lack wisdom, let him ask of God who gives to all liberally and without reproach, and it will be given to him" (James 1:5). What we need today is less information and more wisdom; which is a gift of

---

3  https://dictionary.cambridge.org/dictionary/english/wisdom
4  https://www.merriam-webster.com/dictionary/wisdom

God; and amazingly, the Bible tells us that we can ask God for this gift, and it will be given.

*Ancient Wisdom for Modern Times* comes out of a growing sense that instruction in wisdom is something we should seek and that the ancient paths to wisdom, often overlooked, are highly relevant today. Although times have changed, the condition of the human heart is mainly unchanged.

I have had experience as a son, husband, father, farmer, veterinarian, academic, mentor to business leaders, pastor, and seeker of God's truth. Looking back on my life, it is clear to me that at critical junctures on the road of life, I needed wisdom because all of us are often guided by our uninstructed hearts, which, according to God, are "deceitful above all things, and desperately wicked" (Jeremiah 17:9). This book is an attempt to understand and teach some of the critical principles of God's wisdom from the Bible and apply it to situations that we all face in our daily lives.

I have set out the book starting with my journey, which demonstrates many of the challenges of making wise decisions on the road of life with all its snares, trials, and delights. I have sought to understand ancient biblical wisdom and provide practical solutions for our modern times. Succeeding chapters cover particular areas of life where wisdom can be applied from ancient understandings and made relevant to our day. Each chapter stands on its own and can be read if you are seeking wisdom in a particular area: for example, communication, leadership, money, work, love, marriage, etc. In this book, you will find practical ideas and help to live wisely in a modern world that has lost its way because it has rejected these ancient biblical foundations of wisdom, and more so, the Author of this wisdom.

So please come on this journey with me as we start with my own story, which provides insight into the challenges of foolish choices, as well as God's providence and guidance in the way of wisdom.

# CHAPTER 1
# MY JOURNEY TOWARDS WISDOM

*"Wisdom is with aged men, and with length of days, under-standing." (Job 12:12)*

Compared to the landscape of my childhood—rural Australia in the 1950s—the world today seems so different to my eyes that it is almost impossible to get my bearings and retrace my journey from the time and place of my youth. Today is a realm and a time so changed that I could have lived in a completely different world or planet as a child. It was a time when there was self-sufficiency, isolation, power available only by generator, patchy telephone communication, and hard work for survival. And yet, here I am, living on the same patch of land in the Australian countryside more than 70 years later. So, in some ways, I haven't moved anywhere, and the ground, with its extensive forests of eucalypt trees, remains the same. Yet, everything is different.

While the journey into wisdom is challenging with hard-to-nego-tiate twists and turns, a long lifespan provides the opportunity to understand and reflect on the decisions that lead to life and those that lead to loss. This is the first great law of wisdom, as stated by St Paul in the Book of Galatians: "Do not be deceived, God is not mocked; for whatever a man sows, that he will also reap" (Galatians 6:7). The law of sowing and reaping is a natural law to help us understand that if we are getting bad/painful results from what we are doing, it could well be because we are experiencing the consequences of sowing badly and we need to alter course. I think this book's readers will be interested in my family history and journey to wisdom. If I have any wisdom to share, it is because I have made so many mistakes, but I am on a journey of learning to make better decisions. Hopefully, as Job said, "Wisdom is with aged men, and with length of days, understanding" (Job 12:12), and I will continue to learn. Of course, one of the dangers with length of days is that you can keep on making the same mistakes again and again. Fortunately, pain is a great teacher if we can learn and determine what has caused the pain, and this is a precious gift that God has given to redirect us into the fullness of life.

# Reuben Rose I

My great-grandfather, the first Reuben Rose, seemed to have had a drinking problem. So the family sent him far away from the bright lights of Sydney, its surroundings, and temptations when he was in his thirties to face the harsh reality of rural life in the Snowy Mountains of Australia. The property purchased was called "Boloco" and lay beyond the banks of the then-mighty Snowy River and the tiny township of Dalgety. To access the farm when he ventured from Sydney in 1872, aged 38, it was necessary to cross the Snowy River, which was not easy and had to be navigated by a raft. It must have been a challenging move—about 300 miles south from Sydney by horse and wagon to a sparsely populated, exacting, and cold environment, where the temperature dropped to -15°C (5°F) in the middle of winter. Reuben I (Reuben Uther Bartlett Rose) seemed to have had a good attitude (though it may have simply been the alcohol), which was phlegmatic and pragmatic.

When a wheel fell off one of the wagons after crossing the Snowy River and arriving on the 5,000 acres of land that was "Boloco," he reportedly said to his wife Eliza, "This will do, Mom, let's build here." The site was an exposed rocky hillside about 150 yards from a tributary to the Snowy River, and the location was bleak and faced the full force of the prevailing westerly winds. Somehow, my great-grandfather survived the unforgiving environment, which was dry and barren in the summer and freezingly cold in the winter. In those days, because wood fires were the only means to cook, the kitchen was built separately from the living quarters and bedrooms. One night, my great-grandmother Eliza woke her husband from a deep sleep to shout that the kitchen was on fire.

Reuben I, clearly not a man given to panic, declared, "It's too late to do anything, Mom; let's go back to bed." This quality typifies the Australian character, often described as "she'll be right." For non-Australians, this phrase can be translated as "all will be OK," even when little evidence supports such an assessment. However, this character trait could be genetic, as it seems to have been passed down the line of Reubens (I am Reuben IV). While Reuben I had no interest in hard work, he seemed to have a flair for hospitality. When I read the old family diaries, family members from Sydney always stayed for substantial periods at "Boloco." Reuben I's main occupation appeared to be hunting and fishing and ensuring a ready supply of trout. He is credited with putting the first trout in the Snowy River, and then his life work was trying to catch them.

Reuben I appears to have been a "gentleman farmer" whose hunting and fishing exploits were occasionally interrupted by farm work. There must have been other sources of income that allowed the farm to survive. In the 1970s, I met an older man, Tom Weston, who had worked for my great-grandfather.

"What sort of man was Reuben?" I asked.

Tom replied, "He was an educated man—he could speak Latin, Greek, shorthand—anything!"

Latin and Greek are not great preparatory works for farming, but somehow, he survived and, with little serious farm work, managed to pursue his passions. In the early 20th century, my grandfather, Reuben II, inherited the farm.

## Reuben Rose II

Reuben I and Eliza had seven children. My grandfather, Reuben II, took over the management of "Boloco" in 1905, just as Australia moved from a series of colonies to one federated country. They were tough years with financial hardship and the start of the terrible rabbit plague. Rabbits had been released about 500 miles south in Victoria in the mid-1850s to provide a ready food source to enable the Victorian gentry to engage their passion for foxhunting. The rabbits adapted enthusiastically to the Australian environment and gradually made their way across the Australian Alps to appear in the Snowy Mountains region around the turn of the 20th century. For the next 50 years, the scourge of the rabbit was the major battle faced by landowners in this region of Australia, called the Monaro. The rabbits bred to plague proportions, and there was a devastating impact on pastureland, which provided the sustenance for the leading livestock enterprise—sheep farming. Reuben II was a hard worker and took on the farming challenge, made progress in the battle against the rabbit, and acquired more land in the region.

## Reuben Rose III

My father, Reuben III, became a reluctant farmer after his elder brother Geoff, a Spitfire pilot in the Royal Air Force, was killed in the Middle East near Tripoli in 1943. My father and mother, Kit, married in January 1946. Kit's family were dairy farmers near Bega, on the south coast of southeast Australia. I was born three years later when sheep farming was experiencing a mini-boom. In the early 1950s, during the Korean War, wool became a precious commodity, and sheep farmers suddenly became wealthy (and started paying the government much tax). At that time, wool was worth £1 per pound (and sheep produced about 10 pounds each year).

The yearly wage for a farm worker was about £150–200, so it only required the wool from about 20 sheep to pay the annual salary for one farm worker. Today you would need about 600 sheep to pay the equivalent wage bill. My grandfather died just after I started school, so my father, not a natural farmer, was left to run the farm with my mother, and it wasn't an easy situation. Farming is one of the most challenging occupations, as many factors are beyond your control. It needs the wisdom of generations with the passing on of knowledge to survive and prosper. I grew up as an only child on a grazing ranch of about 8,000 acres and, until I went to boarding school, had little contact with other children. My closest companions were cats, dogs, and ponies.

## Reuben Rose IV

### Trauma as Preparation Along the Road to Wisdom

To add to the usual difficulties of running a farm, my father was diagnosed with a disorder in the early 1950s that they termed "manic depression," but these days is called bipolar disorder. The problem has a range of presenting symptoms, but in my father's case, he would become so severely depressed that he refused to get out of bed for weeks and sometimes months. This was a debilitating problem for my parents. My mother had to run the farm, manage the farm workers, and do much of the work, which in those days wasn't an occupation undertaken by women. Then, with my father, there would be a recovery period when his mood would swing to the opposite extreme so that he would want to travel to social functions, drink, and be the life of the party. This was a puzzle to me and very traumatic for the family as we sought to understand the problem and live with its effects.

Due to my father's mental health (he had tried to commit suicide not long after I was born), my parents decided to send me to boarding school in Sydney when I was just eight years old. My mother became the mainstay of the family, keeping the farm running during my father's depressive episodes and trying to rein in his spending during his manic phases. I returned to the farm by an eight-hour train journey during the school holidays and found that I had an affinity with animals. I became skilled at managing most farm animals, milking cows before breakfast, looking after chickens and turkeys, and riding horses to muster the sheep and cattle. To many, it would have appeared like an idyllic life. However, boarding school was traumatic with widespread hazing, and the "respite" from school at the farm was emotionally challenging and physically demanding. Just as the famous Australian poet A.B. "Banjo" Patterson stated, I discovered that the main aim of the Merino sheep is "to ruin the man who owns him."[5] Life was so difficult at boarding school that even now, as I look back on many

---

5  http://englishprojectdd.weebly.com/the-merino-sheep.html

painful episodes, nothing else has seemed quite as challenging in life since then. So I am grateful for the preparation it provided me to face life's inevitable challenges. The old saying that "what doesn't kill you makes you stronger" is true, but it probably doesn't consider the thousands of hours of counselling required for post-traumatic stress disorder!

Not long after I finished high school, there was such a severe drought that we had to move all 5,000 sheep to a farm that we rented, about 200 miles north-west. I was sent to look after the sheep and bring them in for shearing, which required many weeks of work. It necessitated a 5 a.m. start in sweltering conditions (~40°C or 104°F) all day in the dust, and work wasn't completed until around 9 p.m. At that stage, I decided that it would be wise to look for a career outside farming, and encouraged by my parents, who had received substantial veterinary bills, I enrolled at The University of Sydney Veterinary School.

## College Education

I commenced a five-year degree to become a veterinarian in January 1967. University life was an eye-opener for a quiet boy from the bush who had been educated at an all-boys boarding school. Life became even more interesting when the all-male college I was living in became a co-ed college. I discovered that girls, a mythical species to me, were entrancing, and I also found that they were challenging to understand. University study was rare for most of the Australian population at that time (only around 4% of Australian school leavers[6]), and I was the first person in my family line to attend university. The veterinary degree program was intense, with more than 35 hours per week of lectures and

6 https://www.theguardian.com/education/2016/jun/24/has-university-life-changed-student-experience-past-present-parents-vox-pops

laboratories, as well as the requirement to undertake six months of farm work during the university "holidays."

Even though I was studying the hard sciences, something of the spirit of the age afflicted me with my arts-studying friends speaking of the great value of socialism and drawing me towards equality outcomes for all humanity. I became a left-wing agitator, attending various peace rallies and demonstrations against the Vietnam War. My parents were appalled and wondered about the value of the "education" their son was receiving in the city. Reality, of course, is a great life teacher, and suddenly, I had finished the five years of my degree and needed to find a job.

## Veterinary Life

During my veterinary degree, I became fascinated by the science of veterinary anesthesiology. I persuaded my parents that it would be wise for me to continue as a postgraduate at university and study this new fledgling area of veterinary medicine. After completing my one-year post-graduate Diploma in Veterinary Anesthesiology, I was hired by the University of Sydney to teach veterinary students and tutor in Large Animal Surgery. I spent my days anesthetizing various animals, from cats to cattle, and learning the intricacies of anesthesiology during lessons and tutorials with medical anesthesiologists at the local public hospital. Evenings were spent doing consultations at a small animal veterinary clinic. This year, I met my first wife, Suzette, who was in her last year of medical school. Suzette and I married during the final year of her studies to become a doctor, and upon her graduation, we both obtained jobs in Timaru, New Zealand. We both loved our work in Timaru—my wife as an intern in the local public hospital and me in a veterinary practice, where I consulted on small and farm animals. I had never gone further than the road between Sydney and the farm, so moving to New Zealand seemed an exotic change.

## Academic Life

Remarkably, within a year of moving to New Zealand, I received an invitation to return to the University of Sydney as a lecturer in Large Animal Surgery. I decided that this was a great opportunity, and Suzette entered a training program in pediatrics at the Children's Hospital, not far from the University of Sydney. Although I knew little about large animal surgery, I trained using the "jump in the deep end and swim" method and managed to survive and thrive. I loved my interaction with students but soon realized that the main academic currency was peer-reviewed scientific publications (the adage was "publish or perish "). So, I embarked on a research program that commenced with a Ph.D. On the home front, children started arriving, and it was challenging for Suzette and me to manage two careers and care for our children. Somehow, we survived, and our careers blossomed, and I was promoted up the academic ladder as my publication record grew. I traveled the world giving lectures at various international conferences, and it seemed like a successful life.

## God Calls

When our first child, a daughter, was relatively young, I sensed that there must be more to life than what I had been experiencing, and I decided to attend the local university church. I was surprised to find that the congregation members were friendly and not hypocritical and arrogant, as I had thought in advance. My wife and I continued weekly at the church and attended Bible studies until the pastor asked if he could visit me at work. I was reluctant but couldn't think of a reasonable excuse. He arrived at my office not wearing a clerical collar, which was a relief. After a range of small talk, he turned to me and said:

"What reason would you give to God for being allowed into heaven if you died today?"

To reinforce the question, there was a squeal of car brakes and a crashing sound as cars collided not far from my office.

I sat dumbfounded, and after thinking about my life and the various mistakes and also undeniably bad things that I had done, I said:

"I don't think that I could give a single reason."

His response was to tell me that I had given a good answer. As he left, he suggested that I read the Gospel of Mark in the New Testament, which would help answer the question. I was amazed as, until that point, I had thought that the Bible was something people read passages from at church, but it had never occurred to me to read it myself. I was surprised to find the stories of Jesus, a teacher and a miracle worker who declared that he was the Son of God and who also said that whoever believed in Him would have eternal life.

I was still uncertain of an answer I would give to God about why I should be allowed into heaven, and in further discussions with the pastor, he provided me with a small book, written in 1520 by Martin Luther, called "On the Freedom of the Christian."[7] This booklet changed my life as I realized that I could never justify myself before God and could never provide sufficient reasons to be allowed into heaven. Luther's booklet explained his road

---

7  https://www.elca500.org/wp-content/uploads/2020/04/Freedom-of-a-Christian_final-proof_3.17.20201.pdf

to freedom through what Jesus had done for humanity. Luther's change came as he understood he could never earn his way into heaven. In the booklet, he stated[8]:

"Believing in Him, you become a new person—one whose sins are forgiven and one who is justified by the merits of another, namely Christ alone."

Suddenly I had the answer to the question—I could never make myself right before God, but I could be justified (made blameless) by Christ and His righteousness. This was an astounding fact to me, and my life changed completely. Looking back, I realize that I was acquiring the rudiments of "the fear of the Lord," which the Bible tells us is the beginning of wisdom (Proverbs 1:7). It was a new way of considering the world, with God at the center rather than myself. This was a radical change!

## The Christian Journey—Successes and Failures

Initially, I was utterly overwhelmed by Jesus' love for me, and I sensed that I may need to go and save the world. It turned out that this was a job already done! However, life looked different, as my ultimate hope began to be founded in what Jesus had done rather than what I could do. I enrolled in Bible classes, and my wife and I hosted a Bible study group in our home. I may have acquired the beginning of wisdom, the fear of the Lord. There were the usual challenges of family life. In retrospect, I realize that when two parents are working (Suzette was head of the Child Protection Unit at the Children's Hospital in Sydney), it is hard to keep your focus and attention on your children. The years flew by, and amid the flurry of life and work, we suddenly discovered one day that our teenage daughter had essentially stopped eating and had severe anorexia.

This began a chapter of our lives that was extraordinarily traumatic but, looking back, ultimately character-building. My daughter's treatment involved the whole family and led us to the works of Dr. John Bradshaw[8] on "the family." Among other things, we learned about various family roles and the critical idea of the family of origin. When a couple marries, each person brings "norms" about family life from their own family. This can be a potentially significant source of future conflict. Amidst our learning as a family over 12 months, our daughter made progress toward restored health. However, stress and trauma have their impact in myriad ways, and I had not understood this as we sought to maintain everyday life.

## Leadership and Catastrophe

Around the same time, in addition to my role as a professor at the University of Sydney, I was appointed to lead a research and development program to oversee the government funding of horse research across Australia. This research leadership role was challenging, bringing together researchers from around Australia and developing an overarching national equine research plan. I learned a lot about communication, clarity of message, and strategic planning. At the same time, government funding for universities had been declining, which impacted the School of Veterinary Science significantly because veterinary training is the most expensive of all areas of higher education. I understood that inadvertently, we academics had developed a "cargo cult" mentality, such that we waited for money to "fall from the sky" from the government. When the money stopped falling, we had no idea what to do.

---

8  https://www.johnbradshaw.com/books

Finally, when things became quite desperate and resources scarce, I was appointed Dean of the School. I immediately set about establishing working groups to revamp the veterinary curriculum, find external funding, and reorganize the School. This was an enormous job, and as I worked to increase external funding support, my attention was occupied night and day, such that I failed to recognize the decline in my wife's mental health. The impact on her as a doctor dealing daily with horrific cases of child abuse had taken its toll. She became extremely depressed and eventually was unable to get out of bed.

I pressed on with my work to "save" the Veterinary School, and my focus was not on my wife's health and the challenges she faced. She saw psychiatrists and was given many different medications, but her health continued to decline, and she spent some years in bed. I tried hard to keep the household running and didn't know how to help Suzette. Looking back, I realize that I was trying to juggle many balls but was living in denial. I was emotionally needy and, amidst all this pressure and trauma, became romantically involved with another woman. I knew this was utterly wrong, but as my wife's mental health went downhill, I could not disentangle myself from my other relationship.

One night, Suzette took a large overdose of antidepressants and died. Though I had gone a long way to "save" the veterinary school, I had not been able to help Suzette. Suddenly, I realized that I had failed in every way. There are no words to describe the trauma and pain of Suzette's death on the whole family. Even today, twenty years later, there are still severe impacts of her death on us all and on the mental health of the children, who at that stage were young adults in their twenties.

In those early days after her death, as I sat and reflected on the catastrophic disaster I had created, my pastor from my church visited and prayed with me. He spoke words of life from the Bible, quoting Romans 6:23—"For the wages of sin is death, but the gift of God is eternal life in Christ Jesus our Lord." I could see clearly that the "wages" for all my "work" was death, but my pastor explained that if I turned to God in repentance, there was a way for me to eternal life. It was the unique gift of God that I had discovered 20 years before as I had read Luther's "The Freedom of the Christian," except that now I realized that it was not free. Jesus had paid the price for my sins, but my choices and actions had disastrous results for the whole family. I resolved to cast myself on God's mercy and turn back to Him and put my life into His hands.

Some months later, a Christian friend Kate, who had come to faith in the same church at the same time as Suzette and me 20 years earlier, invited me to visit her at her house by the beach. My daughter, one of her friends, and I visited for the day. While the girls walked on the beach, I told Kate my story of failure and sin as we sat on a large rock overlooking the sea. She listened intently and asked if she could pray for me. Her prayers renewed my hope that God hadn't finished with me, and some months later, a relationship began with Kate that brought joy and a journey of healing.

## A New Life Begins

Shortly after this, I was offered a new professional role in charge of research and development programs for the Australian sheep and cattle industry. In this role, I oversaw the expenditure of around $40 million annually in research funds to help improve the productivity, health, and welfare of cattle and sheep. It was a role that required building a research administration team with a strategic focus on programs that would provide value to the large sheep and cattle sector in Australia. Once again, I was involved in strategic planning, but at the same time, I was also embarking on a new spiritual journey. I realized I had gradually developed a false idea of God and His work. My concept had been that God was very busy running the universe, so, as one of His people, I was like a sub-contractor taking care of my areas of responsibility. I had proceeded in the best way I could, but the result had been a disaster because I had relied on myself rather than God. I realized that I needed to walk much more closely with God and learn to hear His voice and do what He was calling me to do rather than what I had determined by my own ideas. I immersed myself in the Bible and a range of Christian books to help me begin to understand how to hear God's voice. At this time, Kate and I sensed that God was calling us into marriage. So about one year later, Kate and I were married, and we settled into a new life in Sydney, where I continued my work with the sheep and cattle research program. Many challenges continued with the children, but I had a strong sense of God's sovereignty and the need to press into His call on my life.

A few years passed until one morning during Easter when Kate and I were sitting in church waiting for the service to commence. At the front of the old church, on the wall, were two large boards with a large old-fashioned script. On one board was the Lord's Prayer, while on the other were the Ten Commandments. I hadn't read the Ten Commandments for many years. As I read through the commandments, I was arrested by Commandment Five—"Honor Your father and your mother, that your days may be long upon the land which the Lord your God is giving you" (Exodus 20:12). I suddenly thought of my elderly parents who were still running the large farm in the Snowy Mountains. I realized that if I wanted to "live a long life in the land," I had better take this commandment seriously.

## Honor Your Father and Mother

Until confronted with Commandment Five, I had no interest in being a farmer. I had led the life of a clueless academic for 30 years, swanning around the cafés and restaurants of inner Sydney, attending international conferences, and doing what was "wise in my own eyes" (see Judges 21:25). As I stared at Commandment Five, it occurred to me that God's wisdom must be greater than mine. So if I had a sense that honoring my parents meant returning to the farm to help them, I needed a radical shift in life direction.

I talked the decision over with Kate, and with her agreement, I resigned from my job, and we packed up all our belongings to move back to the farm. My parents, then in their 80s, were delighted about our decision, and I had a sense of joy in my heart to follow God's direction. At the time of our move, my father died quite suddenly. I was left to support my mother, whom my father had nicknamed "the Ayatollah," which gives you some sense of the challenge that awaited me. Suddenly I was confronted with what honoring looked like as I attempted to take over the responsibility for managing the farm from my 85-year-old mother. This turned into an ongoing battle with many ups and downs and was a journey of learning and humility for me. As I chased recalcitrant sheep around the paddocks, I sometimes wondered how long my "life in the land" would be! When my mother countered my instructions to the farm workers, I realized that honoring your mother is not easy.

Nevertheless, I can see that simple obedience to the call of God to the Fifth Commandment, to honor my father and mother, changed my life. It has given me experience and understanding I could never have obtained as a left-wing academic living on government support. This season of my life was part of God's training ground for me to acquire wisdom. On the farm, I learned about real work, the challenges of floods and drought, planning during the years of bounty, and, most importantly, honoring my mother.

## Working With Chief Executives (CEOs)

A few years earlier, when I was Dean of the Veterinary School, I joined a group of about 16–20 CEOs who met monthly. The meeting provided state-of-the-art presentations by experts in finance, employment, planning, hiring decisions, team-building, and other relevant business topics. At these meetings, there also was the opportunity to bring a current business challenge to the group of CEOs to discuss and provide advice. The group was called The Executive Connection (TEC), a business started in the U.S. and is now called Vistage.[9]

The CEOs in my group were from varied backgrounds: financial management, engineering, publishing, insurance, employment, executive recruitment, equipment hire, public works, building supplies, health, property development, and others. The idea was that those in the group had non-competing businesses and could benefit from perspectives provided by different views and approaches. I was the first university academic to join the group. My eyes were opened to a completely different world where hard decisions were made, and advice was given without fear or favor. I received significant guidance and support from the group about

---

9  https://www.vistage.com/

some of the problems I faced leading the veterinary school, and the sphere of business opened new ideas for me. Each of the CEOs in the group was generous with their advice and encouragement as I sought to deal with an academic environment akin to a sheltered workshop.

One of the most profound moments came when a former Reagan CIA appointee came to speak to the group about business intelligence. He explained that President Reagan was a great leader because of the simplicity of his focus, which he described at that time as, "Cut taxes and cream the commies!" He provided evidence of the impact this had in the U.S. and on the administration, which was laser-focused because the president wasn't interested in any other areas. This led me to months of work to try to set similar clear objectives for the veterinary school, but try as hard as I might, I couldn't eliminate all the issues to wind up with just two, like President Reagan. However, it was a valuable lesson to me of the importance of simplicity and focus in an organization's mission.

I continued in TEC when I moved to lead the sheep and cattle R&D program, and the group was supportive and encouraging. I learned a lot in many different fields and developed an ability to think strategically. When I decided to return to the family farm, I had a sense that I felt was from God that I should put my name forward to become Chairman of the group. The group decided to hire me, and my work involved about ten days per month, visiting each of the 16 or so CEOs to discuss their business and current challenges. I also chaired a full-day meeting of the group each month. I learned a great deal about asking essential questions and saw the significant business impact of the difficulties a CEO may face in their personal life.

After four years of my part-time farm work, it became clear that I couldn't continue with almost half my time in Sydney and still have time for the farm. Kate and I decided to become full-time farmers, helping my mother look after 5,000 sheep and about 100 cattle. I resigned from chairing the CEO group, and we relocated permanently to the farm.

## Lessons From Farming

I had always thought that it was difficult as Dean of a university faculty where with many tenured professors, you had no employees but only potential volunteers. Academics are very self-focused, and there is an old saying that trying to organize academics is like herding cats. I discovered that this was true. Nonetheless, the role of Dean was much more straightforward than running a farm and dealing with my mother. Many farming decisions have to be made without any information about the seasons ahead, and it is challenging to manage periods of famine and plenty. After several years of running the family farm, dealing with many drought years, and taking food to thousands of sheep, I attended a presentation where an analyst reviewed financial data from thousands of Australian farms across 30 years. The analysis showed that, on average, there were just three profitable years out of ten for farms like ours. I turned to my wife and said, "We've just had three good years!" We started to think about how we could wind the farm back. Not long after this, my mother died, and we decided to sell all the sheep, which were the most challenging work, and 4,000 acres of land and build a new house in the high country of the farm, closer to the Snowy Mountains. The farm now ran about 150 cattle, and I became more of a "gentleman farmer" like my great-grandfather Reuben I. I had more time to think about life's challenges and to understand the Bible better; I enrolled in learning Hebrew, which I have been doing for five years, and have grown in knowing God and gained a deeper understanding of the Bible.

This book began from this vantage point, reflecting on life's experiences and a sense of the importance of writing about ancient wisdom. So now I live on the land bought by Reuben I more than 150 years ago, and it seems like the right time to write and reflect on what I have been learning under the hand of God.

## KEY POINTS—SOME LIFE LESSONS FROM MY STORY

- **We are all the products of families with the potential for problems and benefits from our upbringing and heritage**. It is crucial to be clear-sighted about what has been good and bad in shaping our worldview and to understand how our family of origin has shaped our current perspectives. From the start of time, God's purposes were always planned through the joys and challenges of family life. Sometimes, family pathologies may be complicated for us to recognize because they have become our "norms."

- **Life brings a range of difficulties to every person,** but these difficulties and pain don't need to define us or keep us trapped as victims. However, the problems we have experienced must be recognized and confronted to achieve our potential and take responsibility for our life.

- **We all have a longing for the spiritual**—something beyond ourselves. The Bible tells us that God has put eternity in our hearts (Ecclesiastes 3:11). The great Augustine of Hippo wrote in his *Confessions*: "You have made us for yourself, O

Lord, and our heart is restless until it rests in you."[10] We need to be attuned to God's call to each of us in both the big and small things of life.

- **Learning and wisdom are not the same thing**s. I advanced up the academic ladder, acquired honors, and wrote successful textbooks and hundreds of scientific papers. This knowledge was helpful in my field, but I made foolish decisions as I decided to be "wise in my own eyes." Wisdom has a foundation in God, so the Bible tells us in many places that "the fear of the Lord is the beginning of wisdom."

- **The Bible tells us, "Sin is crouching at your door, and its desire is for you" (Genesis 4:7)**. In this verse, God tells Cain about the danger of sin but then says, "But you should rule over it" (Genesis 4:7). Each of us is drawn towards sin. The results are disastrous because "the wages of sin are death" (Romans 6:23). God's help is needed to resist sin.

- **Sometimes, God calls us to tasks that don't make logical sens**e. As I read Commandment Five from the Ten Commandments to honor my father and mother, I was suddenly aware that the way to do this was to return to the farm to assist my parents. I had never previously considered this idea. I still have a limited understanding of why God called me back to my ancestral home, but I am confident of His call. Oswald Chambers wrote in his famous book *My Utmost for His Highest*:[11]

"The call of God is like the call of the sea—no one hears it except the person who has the nature of the sea in him.

---

10  https://www.crossroadsinitiative.com/media/articles/ourheartisrest-lessuntilitrestsinyou/
11  https://utmost.org/the-bewildering-call-of-god/

What God calls us to cannot be definitely stated because His call is simply to be His friend to accomplish His own purposes. Our real test is in truly believing that God knows what He desires. The things that happen do not happen by chance—they happen entirely by the decree of God. God is sovereignly working out His own purposes."

As we move on from my own story, we will explore together the nature of wisdom as outlined in the ancient writings of the Old and New Testaments of the Bible.

# CHAPTER 2
# WHAT IS WISDOM?

*"The fear of the Lord is the beginning of wisdom, and knowledge of the Holy One is understanding." (Proverbs 9:10)*

The road to wisdom is difficult because there are various distractions and even landmines to entice or blow us off the road. For example, all of us seem to find difficulties in listening to and honoring our fathers and mothers. This character trait appears early in a toddler's life who learns quickly to say no without any need for teaching them defiance. This tendency for independence and defiance in human beings has terrible outcomes, with increases in drug use, mental health problems, marriage breakdown, violence, government dependency, and disregard for the sanctity of life itself. Each generation seems to disdain the ideas of the previous one, and the prevailing modern philosophy appears to be to do whatever feels good to you and remember that there is no truth—only your truth and my truth.

While technology has advanced remarkably even in the 30 years since the widespread availability of the internet, the big questions of life remain the same as they did for our ancient ancestors: Where did I come from? Who am I? Why am I here? How should I live? Where am I going?[12] These questions are often avoided in

---

12  https://www.linkedin.com/pulse/5-big-questions-life-stephen-graves-1c

life's daily rush but ultimately must be faced—often when a significant problem or tragedy arises.

Because our ancient ancestors in the Middle East were not distracted by modern comforts, social media, and endless entertainment options, life's big questions were the sources of much reflection and teaching. In the ancient Egyptian writings, there is evidence of significant interest in wisdom[13] and also in literature from ancient Mesopotamia.[14] The Hebrew Bible has several wisdom books—notably Proverbs, Ecclesiastes, Job, and Song of Solomon. These sources of ancient wisdom, believed to be at their origin from God Himself, will be our focus in this book, and the ideas are as relevant to each of us today as they were to our forebears.

## The Hebrew Concept of Wisdom

The main Hebrew word that we translate as "wisdom" is חָכְמָה (hokmâ), which The Lexham Bible Dictionary[15] defines as "the practical skills associated with living a successful life." [It is important to note that this is success as God defines it throughout the Bible, as discussed in the remainder of this book]. If you look back to the origin of the Hebrew word, the pictographic script shows a wall separating water.[16] The picture conveys the idea of separation, and the concept of wisdom is one who can separate between good and evil. Other words associated with חָכְמָה (hokmâ) are skill, prudence, and shrewdness.

---

13 http://www.per-ankh.co.uk/monuments_of_egypt/literature_and_hieroglyphs/ancient_egyptian_literature_wisdom_texts.asp
14 https://academic.oup.com/edited-volume/34233/chapter-abstract/290260196?redirectedFrom=fulltext&login=false
15 https://lexhampress.com/product/36564/lexham-bible-dictionary
16 https://www.ancient-hebrew.org/studies-words/wisdom-knowledge-and-understanding.htm

# Wisdom, Moses' Teaching, and the Fear of the Lord

The first time the Hebrew word חָכְמָה (*hokmâ*) occurs in the Bible, it is used by Moses in a speech to the children of Israel, whom he is preparing to enter the "promised land." As a result of Israel's disobedience to God and seeking after other gods after their miraculous rescue from slavery in Egypt, the Israelites were condemned to wandering in the Sinai desert for 40 years until the disobedient generation died out. Moses instructs the new generation of Israelites in his speech as follows (Deuteronomy 4:5–10):

"Surely I have taught you statutes and judgments, just as the LORD my God commanded me, that you should act according to them in the land which you go to possess. Therefore **be careful to observe them; for this is your wisdom and understanding in the sight of the peoples who will hear all these statutes, and say, 'Surely this great nation is a wise and understanding people.'"**

"For what great nation is there that has God so near to it, as the LORD our God is to us, for whatever reason we may call upon Him? And what great nation is there that has such statutes and righteous judgments as are in all this law which I set before you this day? Only take heed to yourself, and diligently keep yourself, lest you forget the things your eyes have seen, and lest they depart from your heart all the days of your life. And teach them to your children and your grandchildren, especially concerning the day you stood before the LORD your God in Horeb, when the LORD said to me, 'Gather the people to Me, and I will let them hear My words, that they may learn to fear Me all the days they live on the earth, and that they may teach their children.'"

Moses says in the verses above that the "statutes and judgments" (i.e., the laws of God) are **Israel's** חָכְמָה **(hokmâ) wisdom** and that the other peoples of the earth, seeing a nation guided by these laws, will be in awe of their wisdom and will understand something of the lawgiver—God Himself. The warning is that the default position is to "forget the things your eyes have seen" and turn away from God. To prevent this, Moses says that the children and grandchildren must be taught to "fear" God. "Fear" is the translation of the Hebrew word יָרֵא (yârê'), which means to venerate, to honor, to esteem, to reverence, to stand in awe, to respect, and to be afraid. To fear God is to rightly understand who He is, to place Him at the center of life, to worship Him, and to love the things He loves and has outlined in His law.

Wisdom must start from a foundation of *"the fear of the Lord,"* and various Old Testament authors emphasize this:

The Book of Job notes in Job 28:28—*"And to man, He said, 'Behold, the fear of the Lord, that is wisdom, and to depart from evil is understanding.'"* King David writes in Psalm 111:10—*"The fear of the Lord is the beginning of wisdom; a good understanding have all those who do His commandment."* King Solomon says in Proverbs 9:10—*"The fear of the Lord is the beginning of wisdom, And the knowledge of the Holy One is understanding."* He further notes in Proverbs 15:33—*"The fear of the LORD is the instruction of wisdom, And before honor is humility."*

The fundamental requirement for wisdom is the *"fear of the Lord,"* which results in humility, obedience to God's law, and a departure from evil. It is not family background, the right connections, more education, higher degrees, 50 years of experience, or money but the *"fear of the Lord"* that is a precondition for wisdom. The Bible, in its entirety, provides a clear view of God, who is the "same yesterday, today and forever" (Hebrews 13:8). Unfortunately, most of us do not know the Creator of heaven and earth. If we do believe in God, we often make a god in our image. There is no substitute for reading and meditating on God's Word—the Bible. This means, of course, that we need to know the One who is to be feared. True wisdom is acquired based on what God says rather than what we think. Wisdom will elude us if we build upon the fragile and near-sighted understandings of our own thoughts and those of a "progressive" society. Our lives must be built upon what God thinks and what He says. Only this foundation will establish our lives in the fear of the Lord and wisdom such that we will stand the tests of time.

Moses teaches in the Book of Deuteronomy that the natural human condition is to turn away from God, to rely on our instincts, and not to fear (honor, reverence, stand in awe) Him. In Western societies, children used to be taught to know and fear the God of the Bible, but the teaching of the Bible was long ago pushed out of schools and homes. Any fear of the Lord has been lost and replaced by the mantra, "If it feels good, do it!" We have lost any sense of our actions invoking a rush toward the judgment of God because each person has become *wise in their own eyes, and prudent in their own sight*" (Isaiah 5:21). It is easy to see the outcome of the rejection of the fear of God and His law as Western societies legislate and promote ideas that are in complete opposition to God's law. If God is the Creator of all and has provided a manual for life for His Creation, His rejection will have serious consequences. Thus, it is unsurprising that there is family breakdown, a mental health crisis, gender identity dysfunction, loss of the concept of the sanctity of life, and increasing reliance upon and subservience to the state ("statism") rather than God.

# God Built Wisdom Into the Fabric of Creation

Wisdom (personified as a lady in the Book of Proverbs) was woven by God into the framework of creation from its very foundation. Proverbs 8:22–31 lays this out in a beautiful way. In speaking about wisdom (Proverbs 8:12), King Solomon writes:

*"The LORD possessed me at the beginning of His way,*

*Before His works of old.*

*I have been established from everlasting,*

*From the beginning, before there was ever an earth.*

*When there were no depths, I was brought forth,*

*When there were no fountains abounding with water.*

*Before the mountains were settled,*

*Before the hills, I was brought forth;*

*While as yet He had not made the earth or the fields,*

*Or the primal dust of the world.*

*When He prepared the heavens, I was there,*

*When He drew a circle on the face of the deep,*

*When He established the clouds above,*

*When He strengthened the fountains of the deep,*

*When He assigned to the sea its limit,*

*So that the waters would not transgress His command,*

*When He marked out the foundations of the earth,*

*Then I was beside Him as a master craftsman;*

*And I was daily His delight,*

*Rejoicing always before Him,*

*Rejoicing in His inhabited world,*

*And my delight was with the sons of men"* (Proverbs 8:22–31).

The core of this part of the Book of Proverbs tells us something quite astonishing. God, Himself is Wisdom and a design feature of the universe at the time of creation. God has embedded His wisdom into creation, which is an eternal characteristic of God. He desires for us as *"sons of men"* to be drawn into Himself—His understanding and character. After all, His delight is with the sons and daughters of men. What a remarkable reality—the God of all Creation has built the discovery of wisdom into His handiwork (the inhabited world and even the "sons of men")—because of His delight in and love for us.

In the New Testament, the Greek word translated as wisdom is *sophia*. Referencing the interweaving of wisdom into creation, St. Paul highlights the centrality of Jesus concerning wisdom when He is described as "the power of God and the wisdom of God" (1 Corinthians 1:24). God Himself is wisdom, and there is no wisdom apart from God.

## The Beginning of Wisdom

So, as we begin this exploration of wisdom, some of the essential foundations are:

1. **God, Himself is wisdom, and there is no wisdom apart from Him.**

2. **Wisdom is built into God's creation. It is tangibly expressed and waiting to be discovered.**

3. **We need the fear of God**—"Fear" is the translation of the Hebrew word יָרֵא (*yârê*), which means to venerate, to honor, to esteem, to reverence, to stand in awe, to respect, and to be afraid. To fear God is to place Him at the center of life, worship Him, and love the things He loves. To fear Him, we must seek Him and come to know Him.

4.  **Wisdom comes from God and is found in "hearing" His voice, law, and commandments.** The Hebrew word for hearing is שָׁמַע (šāma') and is one of the essential ideas in Jewish thought. In Hebrew, hearing doesn't just mean listening but listening with intelligence, diligence, and obedience. It is listening and obeying.

5.  **We need to be taught about God and His law** because our natural inclination is to be proud, independent, and *"wise in our own eyes."* The teaching of the Bible forged the very fabric of Western civilization with the principles of freedom and the sanctity of life. The teaching of the Bible has now all but disappeared from Western society.

It is impossible to begin on the path to wisdom without the *"fear of the Lord."* The fear of the Lord is the foundation of wisdom because it requires that we not put ourselves at the center of understanding and decision-making. Instead, we establish God Himself—His character, His law, His righteousness, and His morality—as the foundation of wisdom for our lives. Without this underpinning, we will likely be blown in the direction of whatever is the "progressive" wind of the day. In the Book of Proverbs, King Solomon declares this reality in a wonderfully simple way:

"Trust in the LORD with all your heart, And lean not on your own understanding; In all your ways acknowledge Him, And He shall direct your paths" (Proverbs 3:5–6). The very foundation of wisdom is the fear of God and trust in and reliance on Him rather than trust in ourselves, our ideas, and our understanding.

# Ancient Biblical Stories That Help Us Understand Wisdom

## The Story of Joseph and His Wisdom From God

Occurring early in the Bible, Joseph is identified as a man who grew in great wisdom. The word "wise" is used to describe Joseph when the Pharaoh of Egypt sought the understanding of a disturbing dream (see Genesis 41). Joseph had a harrowing road to the acquisition of wisdom. The second youngest of 12 brothers, as a young boy, he recounted a dream to the family which suggested that his parents and brothers would all serve him. As his father Jacob's favorite, he was already on shaky ground with his brothers. As a result of their jealousy, the brothers sold him into slavery. Joseph ended up in Egypt, but his father believed his other sons' lie—that Joseph was dead. While Joseph had favor from the Lord, he had ongoing difficulties and eventually ended up languishing in an Egyptian prison, having been framed for sexual assault. **It seems as though it is often a hard road to walk to acquire wisdom**. Most of us would have "thrown in the towel," but Joseph's foundations and belief in the God of his great-grandfather Abraham, grandfather Isaac, and father Jacob enabled him to have faith that God would work everything for good (Genesis 50:20).

In a series of bizarre events involving Joseph interpreting some dreams for his prison mates, he is eventually summoned to interpret a dream for the Pharaoh. This was a dream about cows and heads of grain (Genesis 41) that had stumped the wise men and magicians of Egypt. Pharaoh says that he has heard that Joseph was a top dream interpreter. Rather than say yes, Joseph humbly tells Pharaoh: "It is not in me; God will give Pharaoh an answer of peace" (Genesis 41:16). Pharaoh then tells Joseph his dream about seven fat cows coming out of the river and being eaten by seven gaunt and ugly cows. Also, in the dream, seven heads of grain withered and were devoured by seven thin heads of grain. Remarkably, Joseph immediately knew that the dream was one event and that God was showing Pharaoh what He was about to do. Joseph tells Pharaoh there will be seven years of plenty in Egypt, followed by seven years of famine. Joseph also tells him that because the dream was repeated, the event will shortly come to pass. Then, amazingly, Joseph provides a solution to Pharaoh. He says that someone should be appointed to gather 20% of the produce during the plentiful years to store for the seven years of famine that will come after. Then the Bible narrative tells us:

"So the advice was good in the eyes of Pharaoh and in the eyes of all his servants. And Pharaoh said to his servants, 'Can we find such a one as this, a man in whom is the Spirit of God?'

Then Pharaoh said to Joseph, 'Inasmuch as God has shown you all this, there is no one as discerning and wise as you. You shall be over my house, and all my people shall be ruled according to your word; only in regard to the throne will I be greater than you.' And Pharaoh said to Joseph, 'See, I have set you over all the land of Egypt.'

Then Pharaoh took his signet ring off his hand and put it on Joseph's hand; and he clothed him in garments of fine linen and put a gold chain around his neck. And he had him ride in the second chariot which he had; and they cried out before him, 'Bow the knee!' So he set him over all the land of Egypt" (Genesis 41:37–43).

It is a remarkable ascent to power for Joseph from prisoner to Prime Minister, and the story demonstrates several aspects of wisdom:

38

1. **Acknowledge that wisdom comes from God**. Egypt had multiple "gods," but Pharaoh recognized through Joseph's interpretation of the dream and his prescribed solution that the nation needed "a man in whom is the spirit of God" to deal with the coming crisis. Pharaoh had the wisdom and discernment to understand that God Himself had revealed these things to Joseph. Pharaoh realized that there was one true God and that for the country's benefit, it was good to be on God's side!

2. **The road to wisdom may be painful because it often requires real suffering so that pride and self-confidence are replaced by humility and trust in God**. Moses, for example, must have had excellent leadership qualities and intelligence. Still, it required 40 years in the backside of the desert of Midian for him to be valuable to God. It does seem that if we find ourselves in the "wilderness," we should ask God to understand His purposes for us and to learn any necessary life lessons.

3. **Never underestimate the significance of a dream**. Throughout the Bible, God reveals Himself and His plans to people in many and various ways, including through dreams. If you have a dream that seems significant, write it down and discuss it with others who have godly discernment and a history of being able to interpret dreams.

4. **Good leaders are not threatened by wise and gifted people** but appoint them to key positions. In the case of Pharaoh, he had the wisdom to determine that Joseph was a man upon whom rested God's favor and that he was

"discerning and wise." This decision shows remarkable humility when you consider Joseph a Hebrew, dragged from prison with no degrees or credentials but only training in the school of hard knocks. It takes great humility to appoint those more "discerning and wise" than yourself. This is, even more, the case when you are a ruler, like Pharaoh, with unlimited power.

5. **Prepare for the lean years.** Though Pharaoh's dream related to a specific point in time, the years of "famine" are always around the corner if you study financial and agricultural cycles. It seems clear that there are years of famine ahead, with energy and food becoming scarce. It is wise to "store up" resources during the years of plenty to prepare for the famine years. In whatever way we can, we need to have our "storehouses" filled (spiritually, emotionally, physically) and ready for times of famine ahead. As I mentioned in Chapter 1, some years ago, I went to a seminar for farmers where financial data was evaluated over 30 years for many farms in south-eastern Australia. The data showed an average of three profitable years in every ten. I realized that, like Joseph, great care had to be taken during the good years to "store up" resources and ensure a farm's long-term prosperity. As described in Proverbs 6:6–8, making provision for hard seasons is timeless wisdom.

In contrast to Joseph, who went through a very tough apprenticeship to acquire godly wisdom, King Solomon grew up with all the privileges of a prince under the tutelage of his father, King David, who had profound trust in God and "fear of the Lord."

This training ground allowed him to understand that he was not equipped for the demanding role of governing the people of Israel, and when he ascended to the throne, he asked God for wisdom.

## King Solomon Asks for Wisdom

In 987 BC, about 1,000 years after Joseph, King Solomon became King of Israel when Israel reached its zenith of power and influence in the Middle East. It was a time of peace, and Israel experienced extraordinary prosperity during his 40-year reign.

Solomon was only about 20 years old when he became king. His father, King David, had young Solomon anointed by Nathan, the prophet and Zadok, the priest. There had been significant scheming by King David's other sons, notably Adonijah, who tried to take power before his father died. Solomon then took drastic action, acting on his father's advice, and put to death a number of his enemies, including his brother Adonijah (1 Kings 1). Having secured his power, even at the beginning of his reign, Solomon put the worship of God at the center of his leadership.

After being anointed King of Israel, Solomon went with all his leaders and judges to Gibeon, a short distance from Jerusalem, where the tent (tabernacle) for meeting with God was located. Moses had previously constructed this traveling worship center from a divine plan. Solomon worshipped God at the tabernacle and offered one thousand burnt offerings on the bronze altar. He was a man of extravagance! What happened next is outlined in the Second Book of Chronicles 1:7–12:

"On that night, God appeared to Solomon and said to him, 'Ask! What shall I give you?' And Solomon said to God: 'You have shown great mercy to David, my father, and have made me king in his place. Now, O LORD God, let Your promise to David my father be established, for You have made me king over a people like the dust of the earth in multitude. **Now give me wisdom and knowledge, that I may go out and come in before this people; for who can judge this great people of Yours**?'

Then God said to Solomon: 'Because this was in your heart, and you have not asked riches or wealth or honor or the life of your enemies, nor have you asked long life—but have asked wisdom and knowledge for yourself, that you may judge My people over whom I have made you king— **wisdom and knowledge are granted to you; and I will give you riches and wealth and honor**, such as none of the kings have had who were before you, nor shall any after you have the like.'"

A similar account is given in 1 Kings 3:1–15, and from these two passages, there are some crucial insights about wisdom:

1. **Putting God at the center of national and personal life is a winning strategy**. 1 Kings 3:3 tells us that "Solomon loved the Lord, walking in the statutes of his father, David…" God raised Israel as a nation to demonstrate His ways and law. The country achieved great prosperity when Israel put God at the center of life in the kingdom. Solomon achieved peace and stability in the kingdom, and his wisdom was legendary.

2. **Understand the priorities and strategies required for the role that you've been given.** Solomon understood that he needed to know how to "go out and come in" to lead Israel. The "going out" refers to leading the nation in battle, whereas "coming in" indicates leadership in worship as the nation came in to gather together before the Lord. Solomon

had a remarkable blueprint given to his father, King David, for building a temple to worship God. He made this centerpiece of worship the kingdom's foundation, and there was great unity, peace, and prosperity during his reign.

3. **If you don't know what to do, ask God!** It must have been daunting for Solomon to be made king of Israel at such a young age. When God appeared to him in a dream, Solomon knew he didn't have the leadership skills required to lead the people. His request was for "wisdom and knowledge," and in the companion passage in 1 Kings 3:9, he asks God for "an understanding heart to judge Your people, that I may discern between good and evil." We often think we need to have inherent qualities for leadership, but the Bible teaches that we can ask God for the wisdom we need. The New Testament Book of James confirms to us that God delights to give wisdom to those who ask Him:

"If any of you lacks wisdom, you should ask God, who gives generously to all without finding fault, and it will be given to you." (James 1:5)

4. **Conscious incompetence is better than unconscious incompetence!** Everyone will have experienced, at some stage, leaders who are unconsciously incompetent ("they don't know what they don't know"). Bureaucracies abound with leaders who have risen in organizations under **"the Peter Principle."**[17] This principle is that people tend to rise in organizations to levels where they are incompetent. Conscious incompetence (you know what you don't know) is more accessible to remedy than unconscious

---

17  https://corporatefinanceinstitute.com/resources/management/peter-principle/

incompetence. King Solomon had conscious incompetence and knew he needed wisdom and an understanding heart to judge between good and evil. After Solomon's death, his son, Rehoboam, fell at the first hurdle. Rehoboam was unconsciously incompetent; he heeded the advice of his young advisors rather than the wisdom of his father's counselors, who advised easing the taxation burden (1 Kings 12:1–16) on the nation. Rehoboam increased the harsh tax burden; this resulted in ten tribes leaving the kingdom and establishing their own nation in the north of Israel.

5. **In leadership, honor and reward are likely to flow from having your eyes on the needs of others rather than yourself**. When God appeared to Solomon in a dream with a comprehensive question, "What shall I give you," Solomon immediately requested a skill and quality that would enable him to "go out and come in" before his people. God was pleased with what was in Solomon's heart and, in addition to granting Solomon his request, added "riches and wealth and honor."

# KEY POINTS ABOUT THE FOUNDATIONS OF WISDOM

There is much more to learn from the stories of Joseph and Solomon, but I have summarized the main points from the stories of Joseph and Solomon that discussed foundational ideas about wisdom:

- **Acknowledge that wisdom comes from God and seek God for it**.

- **The road to wisdom may be painful,** but the painful experiences teach us about discipline and resilience.

- **Never underestimate the significance of a dream.**

- **Good leaders are not threatened by intelligent and gifted people.**

- **Prepare for the lean years and steward your resources.**

- **Putting God at the center of personal, business, and national life is a winning strategy.**

- **Understand the priorities and strategies required for the roles that you've been given and ask God for His wisdom.**

- **If you don't know what to do, ask God!**

- **Conscious incompetence is better than unconscious incompetence!** Then we are in a position to ask for wisdom about the things we don't know.

- **In leadership, honor and reward are likely to flow from having your eyes on the needs of others rather than yourself.**

Next, we will examine some of the barriers to wisdom, particularly the barrier of pride.

# CHAPTER 3
# BARRIERS TO WISDOM

*"Pride goes before destruction, and a haughty spirit before a fall." (Proverbs 16:18)*

A few years ago, I attended a conference in Washington, D.C., where a business coach who had previously been a Christian pastor spoke. He told a wonderful story demonstrating one of the critical barriers to wisdom—ourselves! This man had taken a job some years ago as an assistant pastor and, after a short period, found himself at odds with several people in the congregation and was asked to leave. He found another role as an assistant pastor in a congregation in another city, but it wasn't long before a similar thing happened. After seeking yet another associate pastor's job, he again had a falling out with the key people in the congregation, and by this stage, he felt very aggrieved. He found himself talking to God and asking:

"Why, God, are there so many difficult people, and why am I having such a challenging time with all these problem people?"

As he waited, he eventually had a sense of God asking him: "Son—what is the common factor in all these problems you have been having?"

Some minutes passed until it suddenly occurred to him that the common factor was himself! This is one of the hardest lessons to learn: we all have elements of our personalities that may be the primary barrier to our progress in life.

Self-reflection is difficult because often, we don't know what we don't know. We all have blind spots that may not be evident to us but usually are apparent to those around us. This is why it is helpful to obtain feedback from those closest to us who can see our faults more clearly than we can. As this is the case, it may be beneficial to ask a few close family members or friends to give you feedback in response to this simple question:

*What do you find most challenging about me, or alternatively, where could I make the most improvements in my life?* It is not easy to have family and friends tell you hard truths face-to-face, but one of my favorite expressions is, "Feedback is the breakfast of champions—but only if you are tough enough to eat the breakfast!"

You will likely find that the feedback you receive will have similar themes, highlighting potential weaknesses or blind spots in your character, and you may be able to take remedial action.

It is vital to become aware of areas in our character and make-up that can be barriers to progress and happiness in life so that we seek God's help to grow and mature in these areas and shield us from what may otherwise be fatal flaws. Each of us is attracted in various ways to foolish decisions when options are presented to us that appear to provide something excellent or pleasurable, even though our consciences may tell us otherwise. Foolish decisions also can be made in response to pressure from friends or family. At the heart of every choice, fear of God (the wellspring of wisdom) must inform and guide our decisions and override our fear of people and their opinions.

# Foolishness

In the Book of Proverbs, the opposite of wisdom is foolishness. There are more than 30 sayings concerning foolishness, all with similar themes. For example,

"The wise in heart will receive commands,
But a babbling fool will fall." (Proverbs 10:8)

"The way of a fool is right in his own eyes,
But he who heeds counsel is wise." (Proverbs 12:15)

"A wise man fears and departs from evil,
But a fool rages and is self-confident." (Proverbs 14:16)

A fool also is observed to "despise his father's instruction" (Proverbs 15:5), and "a foolish son is a grief to his father" (Proverbs 17:25). In a very graphic metaphor, we are told, "As a dog returns to his own vomit, So a fool repeats his folly" (Proverbs 26:11).

The Book of Proverbs helps us to understand folly and highlights the following characteristics of the fool:

- "Wise in his own eyes" and so has no regard for external standards;

- Reluctant to receive direction but rather talks a lot (a babbling fool);

- Doesn't heed counsel;

- Refuses to listen to instruction from his father and is a grief to him;

- Learns nothing from his mistakes but keeps on repeating them;

- Is self-confident;

- Is attracted to evil;

- Is angry.

By default, we seem predisposed to make foolish decisions more easily than wise decisions. Why would this be so? Remarkably enough, it goes back to the Garden of Eden.

## The Obstacle of Rebellion

Despite all our "technological progress," the heart of humanity is unchanged from that of the rebellious couple, Adam and Eve, in Eden. We have inherited the spiritual DNA of our original forbear Adam, who, having been told by God not to eat the fruit of the tree of knowledge of good and evil (Genesis 2:17), joined Eve and ate the fruit because Eve "saw that the tree was good for food, that it was pleasant to the eyes, and a tree desirable to make one wise" (Genesis 3:6) and was deceived by the serpent. As descendants of the original family on the earth, we have embraced this idea that we can be "wise in our own eyes" and live successful lives independent of God.

If, from the beginning, humanity could not follow just one rule, then unsurprisingly, the 613 laws/commandments in the Torah[18] (Old Testament) provide a hurdle impossible for us to clear. One must come back to the central idea that God's intention from the very start was and is to bring us into a relationship with Him, not just obedience to a set of rules, which He knew we were never capable of obeying. The Bible teaches us that God gave rules/laws to reveal the rebellion and independence of our own hearts so that we might learn to seek Him and trust Him and His wisdom as the bedrock of our lives.

---

18  https://religionsfacts.com/how-many-laws-are-in-the-torah/

Looking back to Eden, the narrative of the Bible, and observing our behavior, it is easy to see that we are predisposed to making foolish decisions, particularly related to areas of life where we find things that are "pleasant to the eyes." So we have, at least figuratively, an inherited attraction to temptation and areas of life that can lead us into problems with our choices. To disobey God and to do things our way is rebellion and ultimately leads to death. Fortunately, God is a god of mercy, and He proclaimed to Moses early in the Bible: "The LORD, the LORD God, merciful and gracious, longsuffering, and abounding in goodness and truth, keeping mercy for thousands, forgiving iniquity and transgression and sin ..." (Exodus 34:6–7).

## The Obstacle of Deception

I heard an excellent description of deception some years ago, which stated that the problem with deception is that it is so deceiving! Deception is often so subtle that it resembles the real thing, and it is difficult for us to realize that we are being deceived.

Jesus highlighted the problem of deception 2,000 years ago in a private briefing to His disciples on the Mount of Olives in Jerusalem. Just hours before He was arrested and then crucified, Jesus responded to their question:

*"Tell us, when will these things be? And what will be the sign of your coming, and of the end of the age?"* (Matthew 24:3).

Surprisingly, the first thing that Jesus said was,

**"Take heed that no one deceives you"** (Matthew 24:4).

The Greek word used by Matthew in his gospel was πλανάω transliterated as *planáō*. This Greek word conveys the idea of intentional misleading, and *planáō* (deception) can be translated as *to lead astray, wander from the right way, or mislead or cause to err, form a wrong judgment, get off course, lead away from the truth, or be led into error or sin.*

In this private briefing with His disciples, Jesus provides clear information about the period before His return. He highlighted the issue of deception as the principal challenge facing humanity. Deception will continue to be one of society's most testing matters in the years ahead. The opposite of deception is truth, and Jesus declared Himself to be "the way, the truth and the life" (John 14:6). Thus, a simple way to avoid deception is to follow Jesus.

Woven into the biblical story, from beginning to end, is the issue of deception. We encounter this first in Genesis 3:13, after Eve had eaten of the tree of knowledge of good and evil. Her excuse was that *"the serpent deceived me,"* and the Hebrew word used for deceived is נָשָׁא transliterated as *nâšâ'*. The Hebrew word means *to lead astray, delude, seduce,* or *beguile.* Then at the end of the Bible, after Jesus has returned and Satan is released after Jesus' 1,000-year reign, the apostle John tells us that Satan is released *"and will go out to* **deceive** *(again, the Greek word is planáō) the nations which are in the four corners of the earth"* (Revelation 20:8). I suppose a good summary is **"nothing deceives like deception"**!

The day-to-day trials of deception are part of the fabric of human life in a fallen world, and it is evident from many Bible stories that deception is difficult to recognize. The Hebrew meanings—*to lead astray, seduce, or beguile—help us understand that we are often unaware of deception because it appeals to* or seduces us. We are preconditioned for deception! Deception is at the heart of the work of Satan, who first deceived Eve in the Garden and is described by Jesus as *"the father of lies"* (John 8:44). So—we're set up for deception, and it is difficult to avoid. It seems even more complicated today when governments are suppressing crucial information for their purposes, and we are being deliberately deceived, supposedly "for our good." So how do we avoid deception?

**Imagine an idea or proposal that is against the fundamentals of God's law in the Bible. In that case, it is undoubtedly deception, whether it seems to support a current societal trend or popular idea.** Additionally, deception is likely if coercion is applied rather than free choice. The laws of Western societies were initially based on God's laws in the Bible. Gradually, God's law has been pushed aside in the name of "social justice." God tells the prophet Isaiah, "My thoughts are not your thoughts, nor are your ways My ways" (Isaiah 55:8). Our ways are likely to conflict with God because we are easily deceived into thinking we have progressed and are correct and modern! To avoid deception, we need to know the word of God. We need to heed the advice given to Joshua when he crossed into the Promised Land. God said to Joshua,

*"This Book of the Law shall not depart from your mouth, but you shall meditate in it day and night, that you may observe to do according to all that is written in it. For then you will make your way prosperous, and then you will have good success"* (Joshua 1:8).

The meaning of the Hebrew word הָגָה transliterated as *hâgâ* and translated as "meditate," is essential in this context because rather than the English idea of just contemplating, the Hebrew word has a very active sense and means to mutter, mumble, or speak. It is crucial to mutter and say the words of the Bible day and night and to consider these as the foundation for life.

This is the best advice we can receive today for knowing truth and wisdom and avoiding deception.

**Some other practical advice**—I've read a variety of ideas about avoiding deception[19] and also have found the following advice useful:

1. Don't let anyone "guilt trip" you into decision-making you know is wrong.[20] Our consciences provide an excellent guide to wise decisions, and if someone tries to manipulate us to do something we don't think is good, we need to be resolute.

2. If you ask someone a yes or no question, and the response begins with the word "Well ..." there is a high probability of deception.

3. If you are feeling doubtful, apprehensive, or coerced, don't feel pressured to decide, but take time to be quiet before God and pray for His wisdom.

4. Don't make life-changing decisions based solely on your emotions but use facts as a guide, supported by your feelings. If you have feelings of doubt about a decision, these should be given substantial weight.

5. If it sounds too good to be true, it probably is!

We live in an era where deception will increase, and we must be on our guard. God's Word, the Bible, is our best tool to help detect deception because it is a plumbline for truth, and its principles ground us in eternal truths. When we find ourselves in the midst of life's most important challenges, we have to assume that we have the potential to be deceived, seek God's wisdom, and be prepared to consider a view that initially may seem incorrect. What I have

---

19  https://www.inc.com/jack-schafer/an-fbi-agent-on-how-to-detect-deception.html

20  https://victorythruchrist.org/avoid-deception/

found to be generally true is that opinions that are "modern" or "progressive" are often deceptive, even though they may, at first glance, be attractive.

However, we can not only be deceived by others but can also deceive ourselves. Self-deception is made more likely by pride. Pride implies arrogant deceit—an inflated of who we are or what we know can mislead us into believing something that isn't true—, and we can be utterly convinced that we are right.

# The Obstacle of Pride

The Hebrew word for pride is גָּאוֹן (gâ'ôn), which comes up almost 100 times in the Old Testament. It implies being puffed up or swollen and arrogant—in essence, swollen up with one's sense of self-importance. In Hebrew, the word for pride implies something heightened, but just occasionally, the word is used to speak of God's majesty (see Exodus 15:7), where the same word גָּאוֹן (gâ'ôn) is translated as majesty. In English, the word pride carries various meanings and can imply haughtiness, boasting, self-satisfaction, and arrogance.

Although Jesus did not use the word pride anywhere in the parable he told about the rich man who was feeling pleased with himself because of his full barns, it seems to be at the heart of the story:

"The ground of a certain rich man yielded plentifully. And he thought within himself, saying, 'What shall I do since I have no room to store my crops?' So he said, 'I will do this: I will pull down my barns and build greater, and there I will store all my crops and my goods. And I will say to my soul, "Soul, you have many goods laid up for many years; take your ease; eat, drink, and be merry."'

But God said to him, 'Fool! This night your soul will be required of you; then whose will those things be which you have provided?'

So is he who lays up treasure for himself, and is not rich toward God" (Luke 12:16–21).

Pride is deceptive and alluring. Often it occurs as the result of blessings bestowed upon us by God. It is easy to feel as though we are special when everything we are and have comes from God, and glory should always be given to God. Jesus' parable tells us that whatever we do, we must be rich towards God.

It is instructive to read the story of King Nebuchadnezzar, the great Babylonian king who took the Israelites captive. In the Book of Daniel, Chapter 4, the prophet Daniel writes about God humbling Nebuchadnezzar after Daniel had warned the king as follows: "O king, let my advice be acceptable to you; break off your sins by being righteous, and your iniquities by showing mercy to the poor" (Daniel 4:27). The story in Daniel then says:

"At the end of the twelve months, he was walking about the royal palace of Babylon. The king spoke, saying, 'Is not this great Babylon that I have built for a royal dwelling by my mighty power and for the honor of my majesty?'

While the word was still in the king's mouth, a voice fell from heaven: 'King Nebuchadnezzar, to you it is spoken: the kingdom has departed from you! And they shall drive you from men, and your dwelling shall be with the beasts of the field. They shall make you eat grass like oxen, and seven times shall pass over you until you know that the Most High rules in the kingdom of men and gives it to whomever He chooses.'

That very hour, the word was fulfilled concerning Nebuchadnezzar" (Daniel 4:29–33).

Both these stories, one from the New Testament and one from the Old Testament, point to the dangers of not giving thanks and glory to God, and, notably, the greatest threats to us may come not from our failures but from our successes.

Solomon recognized the obstacle of pride in walking in wisdom and wrote about it extensively in the Book of Proverbs. Here are a few of his sayings:

"When pride comes, then comes shame;
But with the humble is wisdom." (Proverbs 11:2)

"Pride goes before destruction,
And a haughty spirit before a fall.
Better to be of a humble spirit with the lowly,
Than to divide the spoil with the proud." (Proverbs 16:18–19)

"A man's pride will bring him low,
But the humble in spirit will retain honor." (Proverbs 29:23)

The opposite of pride is humility, and the Hebrew word used is עָנָה (ʿânâ)—which has a contrasting sense to pride—and conveys the idea of being abased, submissive, or to be bowed down. Rather than being heightened (a result of pride), humility lowers us and helps us understand that whatever we accomplish is nothing compared to what God has done for us. The road to humility is often challenging, as it may involve failure and even a public fall from grace. God is able to use all the things, both the good and bad, to lead us into wisdom and so into life.

# Some Conclusions About Barriers to Wisdom

The road to wisdom is a narrow one, like the road that Jesus spoke about when he said:

"Enter by the narrow gate; for wide is the gate and broad is the way that leads to destruction, and there are many who go in by it. Because narrow is the gate and difficult is the way which leads to life, and there are few who find it" (Matthew 7:13–14).

Our pride and sense of being "wise in our own eyes" can be the primary barriers to wisdom. We must recognize that the most critical obstacle to wisdom can be our personalities and many character defects, of which we are often unaware. Unless we humble ourselves, we will inadvertently find ourselves on the broad road of pride, which leads to deception and, ultimately, to destruction. Pride is a very dangerous character trait, and King Solomon tells us: "Pride goes before destruction, And a haughty spirit before a fall ..." (Proverbs 16:18). Often, it is a characteristic that is difficult for us to recognize in ourselves. We must be aware that pride may be involved when we refuse to listen to something we don't want to know.

## KEY POINTS ABOUT BARRIERS TO WISDOM

- **One of our major problems in the journey towards wisdom is ourselves**! We need to be aware of our shortcomings and take steps to address these.

- **Significant barriers to wisdom include** unwillingness to take advice, pride, self-confidence, anger, and repeating mistakes.

- **Deception** is one of the greatest challenges we face in day-to-day life. Deception implies wandering from the right way. Nothing deceives like deception, and we can even deceive ourselves.

- **Humility** is a character trait that is essential for gaining wisdom. A vital path toward humility is admitting we need counsel and a willingness to acknowledge when we are wrong.

We have explored some ideas about the nature of wisdom and what the barriers can be. In the next chapter, we will examine how these apply to the crucial area of faith.

# CHAPTER 4
# WISDOM IN FAITH

*"Now faith is the substance of things hoped for, the evidence of things not seen." (Hebrews 11:1)*

## What Is Your Worldview?

Some years ago, I listened to a TED talk by Rick Warren, the noted author of *A Purpose Driven Life*. Rick explained that whatever our belief system may be, "We are all betting our lives on something."[21]

Much of how we see the world and even interpret facts is determined by our worldview. At the heart of every worldview is faith—we all have faith in something we are "betting our lives on," even though sometimes we may find this challenging to articulate. Some definitions of a worldview that I have found helpful are those of Richard Lombard, *"A way of looking at and explaining life and the world,"*[22] and Ronald Nash, a *"Set of beliefs about the most important questions in life."*[23]

A worldview where faith in the God of Abraham, Isaac, and Jacob, the everlasting God, is at the heart of life has become rare in our times as Western society has rejected God and sought to place

---

21  ttps://youtu.be/640BQNxB5mc
22  https://www.worldviewu.org/what-is-a-worldview
23  https://www.impact360institute.org/articles/what-is-a-worldview/

humankind at the center of the universe. A Christian worldview, with Jesus at the center and one where He will return to rule and reign a renewed earth, is a view held by only a tiny minority. However, such a worldview will impact how we see current and future events. Life's big questions can only begin to be answered by understanding your worldview founded upon truth and then determining where you are prepared to place your faith.

In a book from Masters University, *Think Biblically, Recovering a Christian Worldview*,[24] John MacArthur writes that the following questions can be addressed by a Christian worldview:

1. How did the world and all that is in it come into being?

2. What is the reality in terms of knowledge and truth?

3. How does/should the world function?

4. What is the nature of a human being?

5. What is one's personal purpose of existence?

6. How should one live?

7. Is there any personal hope for the future?

8. What happens to a person at and after death?

9. Why is it possible to know anything at all?

10. How does one know what is right and what is wrong?

11. What is the meaning of human history?

12. What does the future hold?

These challenging questions are worth reflecting upon and are helpful for each of us in defining what we believe, where we place

---

24 https://www.christianbook.com/think-biblically-recovering-a-christian-worldview/9781433503986/pd/503986

our faith and understanding, and navigating the times in which we live. It is easy to relegate these critical questions about life and faith to the recesses of our minds as we go about our day-to-day lives. However, eventually, circumstances catch up with us with a traumatic event, the death of a close friend or family member, or a myriad of challenging life circumstances that make us realize that we aren't going to live forever. Muhammed Ali is reported to have said: "Live every day as if it were your last because someday you're going to be right."[25] We need to determine what we believe about the world and what we are prepared to stake our lives upon.

## What Do We Have Faith In?

Some years ago, I was at an interesting lecture, and at one point, the speaker asked people to gather a few others and take a photo of the group. She then asked people to look at the picture they had taken and questioned whom they had looked at first. Of course, everyone looked at themselves first. Social media programmers have well recognized this trait of our self-obsession with "like" buttons, "selfie" photos, and endless posts about "me, myself, and I." This is not a new phenomenon but part of our inherent nature, as demonstrated by the famous saying, *"In the race of life, always back self-interest; at least you know it's trying."*[26]

Self-interest is probably a survival mechanism, but it can also be destructive as we seek to promote ourselves and often tread on others. Behind this individual trait of self-focus is a bigger question: what do we believe in, apart from ourselves? For Western societies, founded on the law of the God of the Bible, what role does belief in God play today?

---

25  https://quotefancy.com/quote/24949/Muhammad-Ali-Live-everyday-as-if-it-were-your-last-because-someday-you-re-going-to-be
26  https://libquotes.com/jack-lang/quote/lbz3f5m

The Gallup organization in the U.S. has been polling for almost 80 years with a simple question: do you believe in God?[27] In 1944, 96% of people believed, increasing to 98% in the 1950s and 1960s. Since then, belief in God has been declining, with the latest Gallup poll in 2022 showing 81% of Americans indicated that they believe in God. Faith in God dropped further when people were asked whether they were *"convinced that God exists"*—with only 64% of people in 2017 indicating that they were convinced about God's existence.[28]

The critical question is: what does faith in something or someone mean? For many of those who say they believe in God, it seems to indicate that God may exist but that they wouldn't stake their lives on this. More Americans have certainty about God's existence than Europeans, but the percentage of Americans who believe in God is decreasing. There are similar findings in Australia, and according to the most recent Australian *National Church Life Survey*,[29] only 25% of the population believes in God of the Bible and that Jesus was Himself God and rose from the dead.

## Implications for a Worldview Without God

The implications for the decline in belief in the God of the Bible are significant as Western societies increasingly enact laws contrary to God's laws. Significant consequences flow from the foundations of a person's faith. Rejecting God results in the rejection of the spiritual undergirding of Western civilization. However, God is not a disinterested party sitting above the firmament but a God to the earth, to which He is intimately connected. God hates wickedness and judges evil.

---

27  https://news.gallup.com/poll/268205/americans-believe-god.aspx
28  https://news.gallup.com/poll/268205/americans-believe-god.aspx
29  http://www.ncls.org.au/articles/australians-views-of-god-and-jesus/

Due to the Israelites turning their backs on Him in disobedience, God judged His chosen people as outlined in the Old Testament. Israel (the northern kingdom) and Judah (the southern kingdom) were invaded, many killed, and the remaining populace taken captive. This was after repeated warnings by God through His prophets over hundreds of years. Specific sins hated by God were the rejection of His law which led to the worship of false gods, temple prostitution, the sacrifice of infants and children, and the practice of divination and sorcery. In addition, Israel was judged for lack of care for widows and children, oppression of the poor, greed, and alliances with other nations who did not fear God.

God cares about injustice and idolatry. These lead to destruction and death. It must grieve Him greatly to see Western nations that previously showed allegiance to Him, His law, and His ways as set out in the Bible rejecting Him and promoting evil laws. The Rev. Billy Graham said in 1955:

*"I believe that every problem facing us as Americans is basically a spiritual problem. Crime is a spiritual problem. Inflation is a spiritual problem. Corruption is a spiritual problem. Social injustice is a spiritual problem. The lack of will even to defend our freedoms is a spiritual problem."*[30]

The consequences of a decline in belief in the God of the Bible are significant for Western society. They are evident in issues as diverse as declining marriage and family breakdown, mental health disorders, gender confusion, social unrest, lawlessness, socialism, economic uncertainty, and even life itself. Western nations inadvertently invite God's judgment by declaring *"what is evil as good, and what is good as evil,"* just as in the time of the Old Testament prophet Isaiah (Isaiah 5:20).

---

30 https://billygraham.org/story/10-quotes-from-billy-graham-on-the-united-states-of-america/

# Judgment Upon a Worldview Without God and Our Response

Most surveys indicate that perhaps as little as 10% or less of Western populations have "absolute certainty" about the God of the Bible and His ways. Indeed, those who hold to a belief in the God of the Bible now are very much a minority. Still, the Creator of the Universe is not seeking validation through votes or social media "likes." God is God, and if we go against Him and His ways, the consequences will ultimately be as shockwaves through our societies as we invite God's judgment.

One of the most famous Bible verses about judgment and repentance is found in 2 Chronicles 7:13–14, where God says:

*"When I shut up heaven, and there is no rain, or command the locusts to devour the land or send pestilence among My people, if My people who are called by My name will humble themselves, and pray and seek My face, and turn from their wicked ways, then I will hear from heaven, and will forgive their sin and heal their land."*

God's judgment is designed to turn us away from destructive ways that lead to death and to turn us back to Him, who is the source of our life. As such, God's judgment is also an act of mercy. When we see drought, plague, pestilence, or war, we must ask: what is God saying about how we behave as a society? God's solution is always the same—judgment is designed to lead to repentance—turning away from our evil ways and back to Him. Repentance is powerful and honored by God, as demonstrated in the response of the king and citizens of Nineveh, outlined in the Book of Jonah.

Jonah initially ran away from a challenging assignment from God to preach the judgment and consequent destruction of the city of

Nineveh because of the people of that city's wickedness (Jonah 1:2). Jonah ended up walking for three days across the city with a simple message from God about judgment and the city's destruction: "Yet 40 days, and Nineveh shall the overthrown" (Jonah 3:3). In what was the most incredible response in history to a brief message of doom, the Bible tells us:

"So the people of Nineveh believed God, proclaimed a fast, and put on sackcloth, from the greatest to the least of them. Then word came to the king of Nineveh; and he arose from his throne and laid aside his robe, covered himself with sackcloth and sat in ashes. And he caused it to be proclaimed and published throughout Nineveh by the decree of the king and his nobles, saying,

'Let neither man nor beast, herd nor flock, taste anything; do not let them eat, or drink water. But let man and beast be covered with sackcloth, and cry mightily to God; yes, let everyone turn from his evil way and from the violence that is in his hands. Who can tell if God will turn and relent, and turn away from His fierce anger, so that we may not perish?'" (Jonah 3:7–9).

This is a template for all nations that walk in evil ways. God is always at work seeking to turn nations to Himself. Humbling ourselves before Him and turning away from evil, from the highest to the lowest positions in the land, is the pathway to God's favor. Leaders have a special responsibility to take the lead in the response. In the case of Nineveh, it is clear that the king and the people realized they were on the wrong track and that God would rightly destroy the whole city if they didn't repent. Jonah's message of judgment changed the core belief system in that great and wicked city. At the heart of this change was an acknowledgment that their faith in man must be replaced with faith in the God of creation.

If we look at the rise and fall of nations through history, God's hand is behind all events to punish wickedness and draw peoples and nations to Himself (Daniel 2:21).

## A Worldview Founded on the God of the Bible

The most precise definition of faith given in the Bible is in the Book of Hebrews. There, the writer says: *"Now faith is the substance (assurance, confidence) of things hoped for, the evidence (a sure persuasion) of things not seen"* (Hebrews 11:1). The writer follows this by outlining Old Testament characters who walked by faith and not by sight. All the significant figures in this biblical "faith hall of fame" firmly believed in something that could not be seen but was based upon God's character and His promises. These stories of faith from the Bible about people like us, with fundamental character flaws, demonstrate the importance of understanding God's character, which is only possible from reading and meditating on His Word and meeting Him in the narrative of the Bible.

Faith is said to be a "substance" in Hebrews 11:1, but in Greek, the word is *hypostasis*. A more accurate translation would appear to be "title deed,"[31] that which has actual existence and in which we can have total confidence. We often use the word faith to indicate the possibility of something, but the Bible author suggests something real—a title deed—based on God's Word and where we place our hope for the future. Lying behind the substance of faith is something quite remarkable: "... what is seen is made from things that are not visible" (Hebrews 11:3). There is another reality, unseen by us, which is tangible although not visible. The biblical heroes in the "hall of fame of faith" "did not receive what was promised" (Hebrews 11:39), and what they looked for and hoped

---

31  https://www.franknelte.net/article.php?article_id=192

in, yet undoubtedly, for them, the "title deed" or "substance" in which they believed was real in the invisible realm and many laid down their lives for this belief. St. Paul says believers are to "walk by faith and not by sight" (2 Corinthians 5:7)—when you see, you don't need to have faith; you only need to believe and exercise faith when you can't see. So, believing (in the invisible realm and the God of the Bible) comes first. Faith is a substance, assurance, certainty, or title deed—as understood in Hebrew and Greek. Faith is the means of our relationship with God—in love, trust, and intimacy—so ultimately, it is confidence in an unseen God and His Word, the Bible.

However, many pressures seek to undermine our faith because faith is a walk of endurance and a spiritual battle. Jesus' half-brother James tells us: "My brethren, count it all joy when you fall into various trials, knowing that the testing of your faith produces patience" (James 1:2–3). The implication is that under-standing God's promises will produce difficulties and challenges, which should be a source of joy for us rather than despondency. This is a shocking statement but brings into reality the impor-tance of the invisible realm and God's long-term plan that we can't see but in which we can put our trust.

So to be people of faith, we need to understand God and His ways in the Bible. Faith is in the future but not blind and without foundation. The foundation of faith is our assurance of God's character, His word, and His commitment to those who trust Him. Amazingly, it is like a title deed.

## Wisdom and Faith

With this background and understanding of the importance of our worldview and the fact that faith, by definition, implies confidence in something unseen, it is not surprising that the world's wisdom is in denial of the foundations of faith in the God of the Bible. St. Paul writes about the challenge of the message of the cross. This is where things become serious because while we can believe generically that there is a God, the message of the cross (we can't be saved by our actions but only by faith in the One who gave His life on the cross), a ransom for many, is offensive and foolish to our natural minds. In his First Letter to the Corinthians, Paul writes:

"For the message of the cross is foolishness to those who are perishing, but to us who are being saved, it is the power of God. For it is written: 'I will destroy the wisdom of the wise, And bring to nothing the understanding of the prudent.' Where is the wise? Where is the scribe? Where is the disputer of this age? Has not God made foolish the wisdom of this world? For since, in the wisdom of God, the world through wisdom did not know God, it pleased God through the foolishness of the message preached to save those who believe. For Jews request a sign, and Greeks seek after wisdom; but we preach Christ crucified, to the Jews a stumbling block and to the Greeks foolishness, but to those who are called, both Jews and Greeks, Christ the power of God and the wisdom of God. Because the foolishness of God is wiser than men, and the weakness of God is stronger than men" (1 Corinthians 1:18–25).

This is a very dense section of Paul's letter, but the key points he makes are:

1. **The cross's apparent "foolishness" is God's hidden power to save us**. Faith beyond what we can see provides an understanding of and confidence in the invisible realm.

2. **The wisdom of the world is deceptive** because although it seems wise when thinking of worldly standards, in

reality, it is foolish. Worldly wisdom is appealing, but God targets those who trust in the world for destruction. King Solomon notes this in the Book of Proverbs 14:12: "There is a way that seems right to a man, but its end is the way of death." In practical terms, this means that if the way of the world, for example, the "progressive" agenda, opposes God's ways, then it is not wisdom but a way to destruction.

3. **We shouldn't look for a sign from God or apparent wisdom of the world but have faith in the crucified and resurrected Jesus**, who demonstrates the power of God. This is truly the "substance" of faith that helps us to walk by faith and not by sight (2 Corinthians 5:7).

## Fake Faith and Foolishness

Some years ago, I read that Prince Charles (now King Charles III) said that rather than being a "Defender of the Faith," a vow taken by monarchs since King Henry VIII in the 16th century, he saw himself as a "defender of faith" because of the multicultural nature of the United Kingdom today. The concept of British monarchs being "defenders of the faith" doesn't have an unstained history, as the title was originally given by Pope Leo X in 1521 to King Henry VIII.[32] King Henry VIII was notorious for his six wives and self-indulgence. Pope Leo X is notable for selling "indulgences" to help fund his extravagant lifestyle and support his powerful banking relations, the Medici family. When one scoundrel gives a title to another, it's impossible to think that "the defender of the faith" has a foundation in the will of God.

At first glance, King Charles' idea to be a "defender of faith" seems to be a noble intention that indicates a desire to be all-inclusive.

---

32 https://stories.sal.org.uk/henryviii/

Whether Hindu, Muslim, Sikh, atheist, Buddhist, Christian, Mormon, Jehovah's Witness, or Scientologist, King Charles will defend you. However, what point is there in defending the indefensible? The ideas and doctrines behind most of these religions are irreconcilable and opposed to each other, so it is folly to try to defend beliefs that cannot be true. Most faiths, apart from Christianity, have a founding idea of earning your way into the life to come. The idea is that you may be able to do enough good things when weighed on the grand scales of life to outweigh the wrong actions. My views until I became a Christian when I was 33 were similar. Having now walked the ups and downs of the narrow path of Christianity (and falling off a few times), the situation is simple but challenging. The Christian viewpoint is that there is only one path to salvation. Jesus said: "I am the way, the truth and the life. No one comes to the Father except through Me" (John 14:6).

This is the perplexing story of Christianity; although this idea is offensive to our human thinking, there is only one way. If there is a judgment day before God and we can't defend ourselves because there is no defense, our only hope is to rely on what Jesus has done. This is why Paul writes that the "foolishness of God is wiser than men, and the weakness of God is stronger than men" (1 Corinthians 1:25).

## KEY POINTS ABOUT WISDOM IN FAITH

- Whether we realize it or not, we are all "betting our lives on something" and putting our faith in something or someone.

- Another way of understanding faith is to describe our worldview, which is a way of "looking at and explaining life and the world." Our worldview is the outcome of our faith.

It will be molded and forged by whatever we are betting our lives on.

- All Western countries have undergone a significant decline in the percentage of people who claim faith in the God of the Bible. The result across Western nations is rejecting God's law and embracing humanistic, anti-God "progressive" ideologies.

- Ancient wisdom dictates that faith in the God of Creation is the narrow path to tread, which is very different from the broad road that the world is traveling on.

- Biblical wisdom tells us that faith requires us to understand that God, His Word, and promises—those things not yet seen—are the reality that undergirds the universe.

- You can see how genuine your faith is because, inevitably, it will be tested, and because the things of faith are "not yet seen," you could be inclined to doubt.

- Ultimately, the surest foundation of the journey of faith is the apparent foolishness of trust in the crucified and resurrected Jesus, who died to pay the penalty for sin for the whole earth and who will come back again.

As we continue our journey to understanding ancient biblical wisdom, we will next explore wisdom in friendship. Just as God calls us into friendship with Himself, so His friendship with us is the basis of all friendships He calls us into with one another.

# CHAPTER 5
# WISDOM IN FRIENDSHIP

*"Two are better than one, Because they have a good reward for their labor. For if they fall, one will lift up his companion ..." (Ecclesiastes 4:9–10)*

Some years ago, I received the best advice about friendship that I had heard until that time. A friend told me: "You have to be a friend to make a friend."

In Proverbs, we read a similar thought:
"A man who has friends must himself be friendly" (Proverbs 18:24).

It also reminded me that Jesus was reported to have said:
"It is more blessed to give than to receive" (Acts 20:35).

Somehow, giving or even reaching out to others brings a blessing back to us. Most of us want friends, but to make a friend, you have to be a friend. What does this mean? You have to make an effort to reach out to the other person, to call, take an interest in who they are and what they are doing, and be personally involved in their lives. Simply—it means to be proactive with the other person so that they know that you like them, think about them, love them, and pray for them. As most of us understand reciprocity, it is likely that the person you are interested in will also start to take the initiative in thinking about you and your life. If they respond to your initiative, then a real friendship can begin to grow, which is utterly different from social media "friendship." Social media friendships have an appearance of engagement. Still, social media is really a tool for keeping people at a distance and preventing real communication, commitment, and involvement in another person's life. Worse still, social media portrays us at our best by editing images and promoting a superficial view of life.

The Bible has important insights into the significance of true friendship scattered through its pages. Most striking is that the Bible speaks of Abraham and Moses as God's friends, and our ultimate aim should be to be a friend of God (Exodus 33:11; Isaiah 41:8; 2 Chronicles 20:7). There are not many people in the Bible described as a friend of God, and to be a friend, you need to commit time to the relationship to know intimately the one with whom you are friendly.

I remember hearing a story told by the Australian evangelist John Chapman that helps explain this idea. Many years ago, John gave a ride to a hitchhiker, and the hitchhiker asked him what he did for a living. John told him that he was a minister of God, at which point the young man said that he, too, was interested in God and sometimes prayed—mostly when he was in trouble. John's response was: "Yes—don't you hate friends like that!"

The story is a good reminder that we often treat God like a distant relative to whom we reach out in times of difficulty and then ignore for the rest of our lives. To be a friend of God, we need to grow in knowing Him and so grow in being interested in what He is interested in and love what He loves.

# So What Does It Mean to Be a Friend?

The Evangelical Dictionary of Theology points out that the "ideas of friend and friendship involve three components: association, loyalty, and affection. There are also three levels of meaning: friendship as association only; friendship as association plus loyalty; and friendship as association plus loyalty plus affection."[33]

Being a friend means having a close connection with another person based on mutual trust, love, care, and support. We grow in knowing the other person—their life journey, interests and experiences, challenges, what they love, and what troubles them. God has created us with a desire for connection with others but a word of warning. Wisdom dictates that close friendships with members of the opposite sex should be avoided. Intimacy creates the danger of sexual temptation, and a wise person avoids close friendships with the opposite sex. Where there is a friendship, this needs to be in the presence of a third person. Many careers have been destroyed through friendships at work becoming more intimate, which is extremely dangerous when either of the persons involved is married.

## Loyalty

"A friend is always loyal, and a brother is born to help in time of need" (Proverbs 17:17 NLT). Loyalty is the key ingredient to a lasting friendship. Many friendships have been destroyed because a friend has been disloyal through gossip, believing what other people have said or sometimes even failing to stand up and support a present or absent friend. Solomon said that two are better than one, and if one falls down, a friend can help him up (Ecclesiastes

---

33  Carl B. Bridges Jr., "Friend, Friendship," in *Evangelical Dictionary of Biblical Theology*, electronic ed., Baker Reference Library (Grand Rapids: Baker Book House, 1996), 272.

4:9–10). Friendship requires that we always think the best of our friend and that if we hear something negative, then rather than speaking of it to another person, we go to our friend and check if the negative thing we have heard is true. The story will often be incorrect, but if it is correct, you can discuss the issue confidentially with your friend.

## Confidentiality

Friendship means being discreet at all times. Confidentiality is essential in friendship (Proverbs 25:9). Most friendships will thrive when both friends know that what they say will be kept confidential—just between them. This is often difficult because when we have secret information, we find ourselves drawn into saying something to others that we later regret.

## Time

Recently I read that to assess your relationships, it is beneficial to tally all the people you could call in the night if you have a problem.[34] The author of this article said that once you have written down the names of the people you could call in the middle of the night, then plan to spend time with them and keep in regular contact. It is easy to take cherished friends for granted and fail to maintain contact in the busyness of life. We must cherish and prioritize time with the friends who are most important to us.

## Speaking the Truth in Love

One of the critical but challenging aspects of friendship is how to speak the truth to a friend in difficult situations. You may think

---

34  https://www.telegraph.co.uk/health-fitness/mind/seven-lessons-worlds-longest-running-study-happiness/?WT.mc_id=e_DM96869&WT.tsrc=email&etype=Edi_Edi_New_Sub-&utmsource=email&utm_medium=Edi_Edi_New_Sub20230123&utm_campaign=DM96869

your friend is making unwise decisions and choices that will cause conflict and trouble for them. What do you do? The Book of Proverbs tells us:

"As iron sharpens iron, so a friend sharpens a friend" (Proverbs 27:17), and also that,

"Faithful are the wounds of a friend, But the kisses of an enemy are deceitful" (Proverbs 27:6).

Friendship requires that we speak the hard things when necessary. Otherwise, we will not be a true friend. If we have to tell our friends something difficult, their response will also reveal the strength of our friendship and whether they are wise.

King Solomon tells us:

"Do not correct a scoffer, lest he hate you;
Rebuke a wise man, and he will love you.
Give instruction to a wise man, and he will be still wiser;
Teach a just man, and he will increase in learning" (Proverbs 9:8–9).

If your friend is angry with you and immediately turns against you when you speak about a complex issue, it is a sign that the friend lacks wisdom and it is not helpful to pursue the subject. A wise person will take rebuke or advice seriously and be pleased to have had your frank assessment. Notably, your friend will know they have someone who loves them enough to say the difficult things and has a genuine concern for their welfare. Importantly, we must also be prepared to receive hard truths about ourselves from a friend if we want to grow in personal maturity and friendship.

## Questions and Advice in Friendship

One of the essential tools for life is the willingness and ability to ask good questions. U.S. leadership expert Pat Murray says: "When you are faced with a difficult situation, you don't need to look for the best solution but rather the best question."[35] He noted that the right questions open the door to insight and understanding of the issue, which then helps us implement the right solutions.

Good friends need to cultivate the ability to ask good questions. I learned this from personal experience in a seminar many years ago. The seminar teacher had us consider a significant problem in our lives, and then we were required to work with another person who would come up with a range of solutions for us. My seminar partner was a man in his 50s with a young family who was struggling to get to the gym for regular exercise. He spoke about the problem at length. Immediately, I was able to think of a great solution and felt very pleased with myself. He was quite wealthy, and it was clear that all he needed to do was to write a check for $20,000 and install a home gym. Problem fixed! As I exultantly shared this great solution with him, he showed little interest and had many excuses for why my answer would not work.

Remarkably, the outcome was identical when the seminar facilitator brought the other eight "pairs" back together. There was not one person who was prepared to implement the great advice their partner had offered. Now this group of people had been together for five years and knew one another well. The facilitator then had each of the "pairs" come back together with the instruction that, this time, we could no longer offer advice but could only ask questions. This turned out to be very difficult. However, it was a highly worthwhile exercise, as the questions uncovered many previously obscured issues. It was frustrating for the questioner, as at various times in the questioning process, one had the urge to say, "Just do this!" The desire to offer advice must be resisted.

---

35  Pat Murray, pers. comm.

Since then, I have continually noted that in almost all cases, the advice we give to friends or relatives is never taken and sometimes is even the cause of real offense. Offense is virtually certain when the advice concerns the raising of children! Though I have spoken with different people in diverse situations, I know no one who has ever appreciated or implemented advice I've given in this area.

So—it is important to resist giving advice and seek to ask questions. Good questions are open-ended and enable the person to find solutions for themselves that they are prepared to implement.

My experience is that asking questions is the best approach when a friend asks you for advice. Rather than providing advice, consider the situation carefully and then ask questions. Here are some types of questions that can be valuable when talking to a friend:

- How long have you been feeling like this?

- What options are you considering at the moment?

- Have you written down the situation's pluses and minuses so you can make a more objective assessment?

- What do you feel that your heart is telling you?

- Do you have a strong sense in your heart about the best option?

- What are your main fears concerning this issue?

- How have you found that you have made your best decisions in difficult situations in the past?

- How do you think the decision will impact the lives of those closest to you?

- If your spouse feels pessimistic about what you intend to do, what are their main concerns?

- How will your decision impact your life in the longer term?

- Do you have a sense of a bigger life purpose? What will the impact be of the decision you are facing about this bigger purpose?

Many other questions can also open a dialogue with your friend, but the questions above are helpful as a starting point. I have carefully noted conversations in various social situations over the last twenty years and how infrequently people ask one another good questions. Questions are vital for friendship to grow.

In relation to advice, I no longer give advice when asked (if I can help it!) but search for a question that may help a friend uncover a solution. The problem is that providing advice is tempting, but it should be firmly resisted since it is rarely taken. A good aim for us all is to become a friend known for our excellent questions. Not only will this approach help us grow in intimacy with our friend, but it also can help the friend delve deeper into their own heart and grow in understanding of themselves.

## Boundaries in Friendship

I was at a dinner recently, and in talking to an older woman about her life, I discovered that she was living in a situation of constant pressure, which had her close to breakdown. An unemployed friend had come to her seeking accommodation, and she and her husband generously gave the person accommodation in their basement. The basement was now a complete mess, but she could not ask him to clean it up because he had told her this was unfair. She was stressed about the situation but felt unable to do anything. In the meantime, another close friend had just undergone major orthopedic surgery, and this friend was calling night and day and crying on the phone. The woman felt pressured to drive the

30 minutes to her friend's place to comfort and help her friend, but she was utterly worn out. She felt as though she was living a nightmare.

Many versions of this story abound. We all have had the experience of feeling used by a friend, and managing boundaries around friendship is challenging. Twenty years ago, I realized that I had several boundary management issues, and I found that Henry Cloud and John Townsend's book *Boundaries—When to Say Yes, How to Say No to Take Control of Your Life*,[36] changed my thinking and approach. It is a wonderful book for readers at any stage of life and helps with understanding where to draw the line about what we are and are not responsible for in our relationships.

I have discovered a simple but essential tool to use when faced with a request from a friend. If you say "yes" to something and it doesn't bring you a sense of life and peace but instead a sense of burden, foreboding, and anxiety, you know immediately that you have said yes merely to please the other person but that the outcome will be bad for you both. If you say "yes" when you know that you should have said "no," there is inevitably a range of downstream events that will negatively impact your life and which can ultimately cause you ongoing anxiety and sleepless nights. However, the good news is that if you have said "yes" when you should have said "no," it is not too late. If you have a sinking feeling in the pit of your stomach after saying "yes," you need to immediately return to your friend and say something along the lines of: "I'm sorry, I just said 'yes,' which I think was out of a desire to please you and be your friend. I sensed in my heart that I made the wrong decision, so please forgive me; I need to reconsider. Let me reflect on the situation more carefully, and I can work out what I can do, and I'll get back to you tomorrow."

---

36  https://www.drcloud.com/books/boundaries

Your friend may be disappointed, but it is crucial to determine what works for you, what you can do, and what you sense is God's leading in the particular situation, which always leads to a feeling of peace in your heart.

It is vital in our lives to determine our non-negotiables in advance. These principles are at the core of our belief system and values, and we should not allow others to determine what these are. We can never compromise on our non-negotiables. If you think that a friend is placing unreasonable demands upon you that bring a sense of death rather than life, it is imperative that you institute changes. These are difficult conversations to have, but they must not be left until you are under extreme stress or close to emotional collapse because then there is a tendency to lash out in anger and frustration that can lead to real and often irreparable relationship breakdown.

## Choosing Friends Wisely

King Solomon provides simple but essential advice about friendship throughout the Book of Proverbs, and one of the foundational ideas is:
"The righteous should choose his friends carefully,
For the way of the wicked leads them astray" (Proverbs 12:26).

This counsel is vital to people of all ages, and it is critically important that we teach our children before they go to school because otherwise, their friendship decisions will likely be quite random or, worse, damaging. The friends we make influence our lives and can often determine our direction and life course.

Both good and bad character is contagious. In terms of bad character, there are many examples of young people going to jail for a minor offence but then becoming career criminals as they come into contact with more hardened criminals in prison. A similar but less serious situation can apply to children at school when they seek to be part of the popular group. There can be a desire to conform to the group and do bad things to be noticed and accepted.

Solomon also wrote:
"He who walks with wise men will be wise,
But the companion of fools will be destroyed" (Proverbs 13:20).

St. Paul supports this idea in his First Letter to the Corinthians, where he writes:
"Do not be deceived: 'Evil company corrupts good habits'" (1 Corinthians 15:33).

If you find yourself in a friendship that is causing you distress and drawing you into doing things you don't want to do, it is best to act quickly and make an intentional decision not to spend too much time or even any time with that person.

It is essential to teach this to our children and understand that something in our human nature draws us toward bad company and sin. At work and in the relationships in our social circle, we need to seek out people who are of good character and from whom we can learn. We should not leave friendship to chance but actively seek out people we can journey with and learn and grow in wisdom. Some of the benefits of making good choices about whom we have as friends include:

- **Personal Growth**—Friends of good character influence our beliefs, values, and behavior. It is vital to surround ourselves with people who are supportive and whom we can encourage and can help us to grow. St. Paul writes these words to the church in Thessalonica: "So encourage each other and build each other up" (1 Thessalonians 5:11). It is always easy to criticize. Still, an essential role of friendship is to encourage and build up, particularly when times are difficult.

- **Support**—Friends can provide support and an ear to hear when we are going through tough times. As a friend, it is important to listen and seek to understand the situation rather than provide solutions. Job's three friends initially did well when they came to comfort and console him after his terrible losses and afflictions. We are told that they sat with him for seven days, and "... No one said a word to Job, for they saw that his suffering was too great for words" (Job 2:13).

- **Decision Making**—At various stages of our lives, we have hard decisions: this job or that job, move interstate or stay, marry or not, etc. Wise friends can help us clarify the issues we face and ask questions that can assist us in making better decisions.

- **Accountability**—There are always areas of our lives that we need to improve. We all have goals for our lives, and wise friends can keep us accountable for important commitments (personal, spiritual, professional, family) that we have made and help us to stay on track.

- **Understanding Impact**—A wise person once told me we can't intend our way into relationships. By this, he meant that none of us has bad intentions, but nonetheless, we can hurt another person with a careless word or harsh criticism. We need to remember that good intentions in friendship are not enough; we need to be aware of the impact we have.

Wise friends can help us understand our impact on others by speaking the truth in love.

# KEY POINTS ABOUT WISDOM IN FRIENDSHIP

- Our ultimate aim in friendship should be to "be a friend of God" like Abraham and Moses. Friendship with God results from spending time with Him in His Word and in prayer, and so getting to know Him and growing in love for Him.

- "You have to be a friend to make a friend" is a saying that we all need to take to heart and implement in our lives. Being a friend means being proactive and engaged in your friends' lives. Remarkably, you will receive friendship in return. "A man who has friends must himself be friendly" (Proverbs 18:24).

- Being a friend means that we need to grow in knowing the other person—their life journey, interests and experiences, challenges, what they love, and what troubles them. "A friend is always loyal, and a brother is born to help in time of need" (Proverbs 17:17 NLT).

- In friendship, it is essential to be open to correction and to speak the truth in love. King Solomon writes: "Give instruction to a wise man, and he will be still wiser; Teach a just man, and he will increase in learning" (Proverbs 9:9).

- When a friend seeks help to solve a problem, finding good questions in challenging situations is better than offering advice. Advice is seldom taken, but the right question can uncover hidden issues and lead to the friend finding their own solutions.

- Friendships that suck the life out of you are often the result of poor boundary setting. When you have a friend making excessive demands, you must carefully explain your life's negative impact and establish a boundary. For example, "Sorry, I can't speak to you in the evening when I am involved with the family, but I am happy to talk to you during my lunch break."

- It is also important to avoid close friendships with someone of the opposite sex.

- We must actively evaluate potential friendships because they are very influential in our lives. Solomon wrote, "He who walks with wise men will be wise, But the companion of fools will be destroyed" (Proverbs 13:20). Good choices in friendship help our personal growth, support us, help decision making, and provide accountability.

In the next chapter of our journey towards wisdom, we will examine the area of wisdom in communication, which is at the heart of all relationships, including those with our family and friends.

# CHAPTER 6
# WISDOM IN COMMUNICATION

*"Pleasant words are like a honeycomb,*
*Sweetness to the soul and health to the bones."*
*(Proverbs 16:24)*

Communication is a daily area of challenge for everyone. We often speak hastily and then regret what we have said. Equally important is non-verbal communication, and many studies have found that body language and tone of voice can be more critical in face-to-face communication than the actual words spoken. Undoubtedly there are new complexities in communication in the age of Zoom and other online forms of communication. However, there is a high chance of misunderstanding whatever the form of communication.

Some years ago, in a presentation about leadership, the speaker identified one of the most critical issues: communication. His quote from a professor of communication at UCLA was, "The result of all communication is misunderstanding!" In the 20 years since I heard this presentation, I have noted over and over again how true this is. No matter how hard we try, we often find that the people we communicate with hear something quite different from what we thought we said. This issue has been magnified since the advent of text messages, social media, and email, where miscommunication is even more likely. However, even in verbal communication, we can pick up messages quite different from what we actually heard. All of us have dealt with someone who says, "I am fine," when everything about them tells you they are not. We are often quick to ascribe bad intentions to what others have said but easily assign good intentions to our own communications. These are essential issues to consider in our communication and others' communication with us.

Ancient wisdom from the Bible provides great perspectives on communication that are still relevant in the modern world, even where digital messaging has become the usual mode. In this chapter, I have attempted to distil some of the Bible's most important ideas on communication.

## Speak the Truth in Love

In the letter to the Ephesians (4:15–16), St. Paul writes:
"… speaking the truth in love, you may grow up in all things into Him who is the head—Christ— from whom the whole body, joined and knit together by what every joint supplies, according to the effective working by which every part does its share, causes growth of the body for the edifying of itself in love."

St. Paul highlights the image of believers being part of a whole-body system, with Christ as the head. The focus is on Christian believers working together to express different gifts, but the verse's core—"speaking the truth in love"—is relevant to our broader communications. At first glance, this looks simple, but it is much more complicated than we would like. We all know people who speak the truth, at least as far as they see it, but leave behind them a trainwreck of relationships. Their view would be: "Well, I just say it how it is." People like this place a high value on truth, or their view of truth, but not a high value on relationships.

In contrast, some err in the opposite direction by speaking with "love" but avoiding the truth. They want to dodge conflict and speak to affirm others and avoid telling the truth. The challenge is to speak truth and love together, which is often tricky because the truth may mean saying something tough. However, speaking the truth in love means finding a way to talk to another person about something challenging so that they realize that you have their welfare in mind and are attentive to their needs and feelings. This is not easy and is made more difficult because there are some to whom we speak who have no desire to hear the truth. It's like the scene in the film *A Few Good Men*,[37] where in the courtroom, the prosecutor says, "I want the truth," and the witness then declares, "You can't handle the truth." Often, many people are not ready for the truth, ourselves included.

## Speaking the Truth in Love: When to Speak and When Not to Speak

Because many of us find it difficult to handle the truth, the Book of Proverbs tells us that we must exercise discernment in our communications.

"Do not correct a scoffer, lest he hate you;

Rebuke a wise man, and He will love you;

Give instruction to a wise man, and he will be still wiser;

Teach a just man, and he will increase in learning." (Proverbs 9:8–9)

---

37  https://www.imdb.com/title/tt0104257/

We don't hear the word "scoffer" very often these days, but Proverbs provides more definition and understanding of the word "scoffer" later in the book where we are told:

"A proud and haughty man—'Scoffer' is his name;
He acts with arrogant pride" (Proverbs 21:24).

A scoffer is a proud, arrogant, or haughty person, and the Bible tells us that speaking to someone like this is useless. In what seems to be a similar vein, Jesus said not to "cast your pearls before swine" (Matthew 7:6). Bringing people valuable words is not always called for, even if they need to year them. We can find ourselves being the subject of the "shoot the messenger" syndrome, where the person delivering the message becomes the target so that the message can be avoided.

The main point here is that while it is essential to speak the truth in love, we must also be shrewd about when we speak and remain silent.

# When People Don't Speak the Truth

The opposite of speaking the truth is to speak falsely, and we all have found ourselves in certain situations where, as a friend of mine says, "I had to lie more than I would have liked!"

King Solomon puts God's perspective into view in Proverbs 6:16–19:

"These six things the LORD hates,
Yes, seven are an abomination to Him:
A proud look,
A lying tongue,
Hands that shed innocent blood,
A heart that devises wicked plans,

Feet that are swift in running to evil,

A false witness who speaks lies,

And one who sows discord among brethren."

Wickedness, evil, and murder could be anticipated as things that the Lord hates, but it is interesting to find, and it tells us much about God, that pride, lying, perjury, and creating division are in God's top seven "hates." Interestingly, these four often are linked: pride can result in lying to protect our perceived reputation. To further protect ourselves, it is a small step to perjury so that the truth is not discovered. Then the proud person can distract attention from their failings by sowing discord and division in our social groups or work settings. Proverbs also provide further advice about the person who sows discord and is a "talebearer":

"He who goes about as a talebearer reveals secrets;

Therefore do not associate with one who flatters with his lips" (Proverbs 20:19).

A person who reveals other people's secrets often is a flatterer and should be avoided. This ancient advice is crucial as it is easy to be deceived by a flatterer who intends to make themselves look good. If we associate with such a person, we end up being influenced by their behavior and are also likely to develop some of their characteristics.

## The Power of Words

As we think about how to communicate and the various traps we can fall into along the way, there is a thread of wisdom about communication that runs through the Book of Proverbs and can be of great assistance if we can be aware of what we say and if we practice.

1. **Don't speak words that cut or harm.**
   "There is one who speaks like the piercings of a sword,
   But the tongue of the wise promotes health." (Proverbs 12:18)

2. **Choose a "soft" answer rather than a harsh one**.
   "A soft answer turns away wrath,
   But a harsh word stirs up anger." (Proverbs 15:1)

3. **Speak gracious and pleasant words that bring life and health**.
   "Pleasant words are like a honeycomb,
   Sweetness to the soul and health to the bones." (Proverbs 16:24)

4. **With knowledge and even temper comes restraint**.
   "He who has knowledge spares his words,
   And a man of understanding is of a calm spirit." (Proverbs 17:27)

5. **The tongue has the power to bring death or life**.
   "Death and life are in the power of the tongue,
   And those who love it will eat its fruit." (Proverbs 18:21)

All these verses in Proverbs provide simple and practical instruction about how we should speak to others, and we can practice these and grow in awareness of the impact of our words. These verses all point to the effect that our words can have on others. We are likely to speak cutting or harmful words when provoked or angry. These are the times that we need to pause and look for a pleasant or soft word that is true but can be like a balm and soothe a troubled situation.

Jesus was more severe in his teaching about the power of our words. He said:

"... that for every idle word men may speak, they will give account of it in the day of judgment. For by your words you will be justified, and by your words, you will be condemned" (Matthew 12:36–37).

This is chastening to us all and a reminder that we need to be extremely careful with our words and cautious not to speak idly.

# Effective Listening and Hearing

It is difficult for us to listen and hear. This is not because hearing problems are widespread but because it seems that part of our fallen human makeup makes us reluctant to hear. Jesus, both before and after His death, drew attention to this. One of his most frequently used expressions after he had given an important teaching was, "He who has ears to hear, let him hear" (Matthew 11:15, Matthew 13:9, Matthew 13:43, Mark 4:9, Mark 4:23, Mark 7:16, Luke 8:8, Luke 14:35, Revelation 2:7, Revelation 2:11, Revelation 2:17, Revelation 2:29, Revelation 3:6, Revelation 3:13, Revelation 3:22, Revelation 13:9). It seems as though we are likely to have an inherent hearing blockage such that we don't want to hear some things and often have difficulty in listening to what is really being said.

These are some helpful ideas that I have found useful to assist in hearing and listening:

- **It is essential always to give your full attention to the speaker**. I need to keep reminding myself of this, especially with my wife, as I tend to guess what she will say and then tune out as I think about my response. Mostly I am wrong!

- **Don't interrupt**. This is one of the most frustrating things for the person you are talking to. It usually occurs because you have a sense of urgency to respond, but you need to wait and listen to fully understand what the other person is saying before responding.

- **Non-verbal listening cues** such as nodding and showing interest and concentration can be helpful to the other person for them to know that you are engaged with what they are telling you.

- **Active listening is always helpful, such as rephrasing or clarifying the other person's words**. Phrases like "I think that what you are saying is ..." or "Did I understand you correctly when you said ..."

- **Avoid multitasking,** particularly when you are on the phone. This is a note to myself as I often prepare food or do other tasks rather than being fully present in the conversation.

# Being a Person of Your Word

Jesus spoke simply about the matter of our words when dealing with making oaths to do or not to do something, which was an important issue of the day. Jesus said:

"Let your Yes be simply Yes, and your No be simply No" (Matthew 5:37, Amplified Bible). This idea is reiterated by the apostle James who says, "But let your 'Yes' be 'Yes,' and your 'No,' 'No,' lest you fall into judgment ..." (James 5:12).

Making oaths is not part of modern culture, but it is interesting that, speaking to business people who were active in commerce in the 1950s, there was a time when your word was your bond. These days appear to have passed into history, but for each of us, the challenge is to keep our word and to be a person whose "yes" and "no" can be trusted.

In most cases, our lives are defined by what we say "no" to. If we say "yes" all the time, it results in others dictating our lives, and we become blown about by the winds of other people's lives and circumstances. Your satisfaction in life may be determined by what you say "no" to more than what you say "yes" to. A talk by a business coach I heard some years ago had a significant impact when he put forward this statement: we must work out our non-negotiables. These are the areas that we have determined where we will not compromise. It may be a boss pressuring us to do something unethical, or it may simply be an area of our personal life where we have determined to stand our ground.

Many people have never set out to determine their non-negotiables intentionally, and so, in various situations, they find that they do whatever it takes to achieve the desired outcome. After making a series of decisions based on no firm foundation, the person can descend into a moral morass. Each of us needs to determine, in advance, what we say "yes" and "no" to.

As I described in the chapter on friendship, my experience is that when we say "yes" to something, and we immediately have a sense of dread or feeling that we have done the wrong thing, we need to take a courageous stand and immediately tell the other person we have made a bad decision. We usually have said "yes" out of fear of causing offense or being viewed as selfish or difficult. Suppose you don't act immediately to reverse your decision in these circumstances. In that case, the situation will continue to trouble you and invariably lead to outcomes that can be negative for you and others. This often occurs, for example, when a superior at work asks you to do something that you don't have the time or skills to do. You say yes out of pressure and a desire to please rather than being prepared to discuss with your superior why you cannot take on the project.

## Pitfalls in Electronic Communication

In ancient times, only a few people could write or even had the necessary materials. Great care was taken with ancient scrolls, and the Jewish scribes who wrote the Old Testament took extreme measures to avoid and deal with mistakes. One mistake meant the whole manuscript was destroyed, and the writer started again. The advent of the printing press 500 years ago changed everything, making written communication more straightforward and accessible.

The advent of personal computers brought a further revolution in communication. I remember the change clearly because, in the university department where I worked, two secretaries would type up documents, corrections would be made, and then the documents would be retyped. One day, an Apple IIe computer arrived, and some weeks later, I found I could type and edit documents myself. About ten years later, email was introduced, and suddenly, messages were arriving in great numbers, and everyone's jobs seemed to morph into answering emails rather than doing any real work. Ten years later, social media arrived with text messages, Facebook, Twitter, WhatsApp, Instagram, and other communication applications. Suddenly, you could connect with many people instantaneously and express your views without any filter. Not surprisingly, this has led to many problems, including bullying and harassment, and censorship of speech. Individuals have been targeted for having unacceptable views, whereas 20 years ago, these views would only have been expressed to a small circle of friends and colleagues. Extraordinary care is needed in using any digital communication, such as social media and email. Communication can live forever in the digital universe.

Many people fail to understand that when signing up for "free" social media sites, their privacy is also being signed away. As the saying goes, "When something is free, it means that you are the product!"

My wife is very wise, and despite having no computer training, she has excellent instincts. When Facebook became widely used about 2005, I was going to hand over all my information to set up an account. She said:

*"Don't do it—they are after all your data, and you'll have no privacy."*

Some years later, there was much publicity that Facebook was doing just as she said, and I was glad that I never signed up for the platform.

Then a little later, I bought an Amazon Echo device, and I had just set it up in the house and was calling out—

*"Alexa, what's the temperature,"* *"Alexa, play Bob Dylan's latest album,"* and other great commands when my wife walked in.

*"What's that?"* she asked.

*"It's Alexa doing all sorts of cool stuff just by me talking to her,"* I exclaimed. "I ask her a question, then she connects to the internet and finds the answer or plays the music I've asked for."

My wife did not hesitate but reached straight into her nuclear arsenal:

*"Right! It's either Alexa or me,"* she said.

I hesitated for 30 seconds, long enough for my wife to know it was a hard decision. I loved Alexa and what she could do for me. However, I realized that I held no cards, so I packed up Alexa and sent her off to a friend in the U.S. He knew why I sent Alexa to him. Still, he used the device for several years until he realized the extent to which Alexa was spying on him and threw the device out.

These stories are important because, undoubtedly, there will be a continuous stream of successive generations of social media tools that ensnare the user and provide extensive personal data to technology giants. Many people seem content to have no data privacy but undoubtedly will live to regret handing over information that should be private and can be used against them. Email also is a potential trap, although most young people no longer use email but other social media platforms like Instagram. However, email is still the main application for communication in business, and after making several significant communication errors, here are my top email/electronic communication tips:

- **Making a phone call or seeing someone face-to-face is the best communication strategy in challenging situations**. It is easier and simpler to send a text or an email, but in any situation that involves emotion, it is best to pick up the phone and seek clarity and understanding. It is even better to go to the other person and have a conversation. The worst of all possibilities is having this conversation publicly or raising the issue in a public meeting.

- **Remember that nothing in electronic communication is private**. It is interesting to see the various text messages and emails that have come to light over the past 20 years involving multiple scandals because of unguarded communication. It is worthwhile remembering the advice of an old boss of mine: "Don't write anything in an email or text that you would feel embarrassed to see on the front page of a newspaper." Dispense with "free" email and pay for subscriptions to reputable organizations that provide an encrypted and private email.

- **Take yourself off social media**. These applications are addictive, and enormous amounts of time can be wasted. Additionally, people tend to share much personal information about themselves that, in the wrong hands, can be used against them in various ways. This advice may be like trying to shut the stable door after the horse has escaped, but I know people who have taken themselves off social media and found that their lives and those of their families are immeasurably improved.

- **If you are angry or emotional in any way, don't respond by email or text** to the person who has been the cause of your emotion. A good piece of advice I heard some years ago was that if you felt compelled to send an email in such a situation, send it to yourself. However, even doing this is dangerous because the email may come to light. I have seen situations that were not serious until an inflammatory email was received, and then it was as though World War III had erupted. The email had been forwarded to others, and suddenly, many relationships were irretrievably damaged, and there was no road back. It is very tempting to send an email when you feel hurt or angry, but there is only a tiny window of satisfaction as you hit "send." The sense of satisfaction is brief before you experience a world of pain.

- **With emails, take care with "reply to all."** I have inadvertently done this because I was in a hurry and failed to realize I was sending a message to dozens of people. The reply to all tool in email software can be very dangerous and cause many difficulties for you and should be used very sparingly.

# KEY POINTS ABOUT WISDOM IN COMMUNICATION

- **Speak the truth in love**. This is difficult for all of us as our motivations are sometimes hidden, even from ourselves. It is essential not just to speak the truth (which can be hurtful) or to speak only in what we think is love (which can avoid the truth) but to speak the truth in love. It is never possible to speak in love if we are withholding the truth. Love and truth go together. This means simply treating another person as you would want to be treated. This general rule is good, but each person is different, and some are more sensitive than others. It is always good to take into account an understanding of their personality and how they communicate when you speak the truth in love.

- **Use discernment in speaking the truth**. Those who are wise are pleased to hear the truth, but fools and scoffers will not only reject the truth but may turn on you and seek revenge. The Book of Proverbs tells us, "Do not correct a scoffer, lest he hate you; Rebuke a wise man, and he will love you. Give instruction to a wise man, and he will be still wiser; Teach a just man, and he will increase in learning" (Proverbs 9:8–9).

- **Let your "yes" be yes and "no" no**. Being reliable and a person whose word can be trusted is of great value and enables you to be known as someone trustworthy.

- **A pleasant or soft word can turn away anger in a difficult situation (Proverbs 16:24).** This is the most difficult thing to carry out because we primarily respond out of the emotion we feel. Nonetheless, it is invariably beneficial to the situation and relationship.

- **"The result of all communication is misunderstanding."**[38] It is worthwhile remembering that no matter how effective a communicator you are, misunderstanding is often likely to be the result, especially if it is complex or sensitive subject matter. You need to check in about what people have heard in response to an important message.

- **Take care with all electronic communication, and never send an email or text when you are angry**. It's worthwhile remembering that no electronic communication is private and that emails and texts can end up being widely distributed to many others and come back to haunt you.

At this stage in our exploration of ancient wisdom, we move on from wisdom in communication to wisdom in conflict. The saying that all communication leads to misunderstanding highlights the fact that conflict often is the inadvertent outcome of our communication, and we need to be aware of this possibility in our communications.

---

38  Pat Murray, pers comm

# CHAPTER 7
# WISDOM IN CONFLICT

*"A soft answer turns away wrath, but a harsh word stirs up anger." (Proverbs 15:1)*

It is difficult to escape from conflict in life, and when we do escape, often it is because we are avoiding facing up to a problematic issue or a challenging person. Jesus' half-brother James wrote the most straightforward biblical approach to conflict, and it is a verse that we need to keep close to our hearts: "So then, my beloved brethren, let every man be swift to hear, slow to speak, slow to wrath; for the wrath of man does not produce the righteousness of God" (James 1:19–20).

James' prescription for life, particularly when facing various trials and difficulties, is being ready to listen while being slow to speak or become angry. Unfortunately, we mostly invert this great advice and find ourselves being slow to hear, quick to speak, and quick to become angry.

## Implementing James' Advice About Listening, Speaking, and Being Angry

### Be Swift to Hear
Some years ago, I attended a course on leadership and conflict. The course leaders taught the importance of listening, and I

discovered first-hand how important this is. Another person on the course had taken offense to me in a situation that I thought was relatively minor, but he was furious. His face turned red, and the veins in his neck stood out.

"Can you tell me how you are feeling?" I asked.

I thought he was going to explode, and he replied, "I haven't felt so angry since I was ten years old, and my father treated me the same way you did."

I realized that I had stumbled into challenging territory, but with the help of the course leaders, I was able to say:

"I'm so sorry—tell me more."

He explained that when we had spoken earlier about an incident that I had brought up to the group, he had apologized, but I had crossed my arms, and this gesture appeared hostile to him. My response reminded him of his father, who used to do the same thing. I continued to ask if there was more that was bothering him, and he spoke about various things in our interaction that had triggered his anger. My first instinct was to try to explain myself and to say that I didn't mean to upset him, but I held off and listened and continued to ask: "Is there more?" The process took about 20 minutes as the group members looked on and squirmed in their seats. I discovered a few critical things:

1. Simply listening and asking questions to help you understand have a profound impact, even when you cannot "fix" the situation.

2. Even though I thought that he had dramatically overreacted to me, asking questions and listening helped me understand why he had reacted the way he did, resulting in empathy toward him. With coaching from the course

leadership, I could listen and ask questions that helped us both understand, and the outcome was the restoration of the relationship.

I gained direct experience of the importance of Stephen Covey's quote: "Seek first to understand, then to be understood."[39] One of the course facilitators told me something that has been helpful ever since. He said, "A person's reaction to something you did tells you a lot about them and nothing about you." Mostly, we don't realize this, but if something you say "triggers" another person, it tells you that you have uncovered previous pain and difficulty unrelated to you, even though the anger often feels personally directed.

The Book of Proverbs once again has timely advice:
"He who gives an answer before he hears,
It is folly and shame to him" (Proverbs 18:13).

We all have problems stilling our minds and listening when in a conflict. We usually are busy formulating our defense and what we will say rather than intentionally listening and understanding.

Even though I learned an important lesson that day, I still find it challenging when I am misunderstood or in a situation of conflict. I have noticed the same problem with the behavior of others. Faced with unjust accusations, we seek to justify, explain, and defend (JED) ourselves rather than listen, ask questions, and increase our understanding. It's important to make a mental note to ourselves that if we are "jedding" (justifying, explaining, and defending), we need to stop, listen, and ask questions, demonstrating that we are interested in the other person and what they have to say.

---

39  https://resources.franklincovey.com/the-7-habits-of-highly-effective-people/habit-5-seek-first-to-understand-then-to-be-understood

Husbands are noted for having an insufficient capacity for listening to their wives. Many marriages could be improved through the simple process of listening rather than trying to defend ourselves. Even as I write this, I realize it is advice I must take myself!

## Be Slow to Speak

The second part of James' advice is to be slow to speak. Personally, I find this extremely difficult, but those who are introverts (those who get their energy from the inner world) in the Myers-Briggs Type Indicators (MBTI)[40] will tend to need time to process what they hear before they are ready to speak. Slowness to speak can be difficult and stressful for extroverts (those who get their energy from the external environment). No matter what personality type you are, it is important to be slow to speak in situations that may involve conflict and are stressful. Hastiness and anger can result in us saying something that can be hard to withdraw but can have a long-term negative impact.

I recently met a young woman whose mother had said, "I hate you" some years before. Just three words, but these words deeply impacted the woman's life and have taken a massive toll on her emotional health.

The Book of Proverbs tells us:
"Even a fool is counted wise when he holds his peace;
When he shuts his lips, he is considered perceptive" (Proverbs 17:28).

What an incredible idea—we can be considered wise by not saying anything! It could just be worthwhile trying this approach for a few weeks to see the impact. One of the observations I have made over

---

40  https://www.themyersbriggs.com/en-US/Products-and-Services/My-ers-Briggs

the years is that good listeners are rare. Being prepared to listen to people and ask open-ended questions rather than providing opinions can have a remarkably beneficial effect on relationships. It is certainly powerful, although challenging to do, especially in a situation where there is conflict.

## Be Slow to Anger

Anger is seldom justified and can be profoundly destructive. James tells us to be "slow to wrath," but this is not as easy as it seems. We all have areas in life where our emotions are "triggered," and when this happens, it is crucial to seek an understanding of what lies behind the circumstances that "trigger" us to anger. Often, there is an antecedent long before in our childhood, and we can need help to determine the origin of emotions that are stirred up from past events.

The Book of Proverbs has a simple but profound formula for us:
"A soft answer turns away wrath,
But a harsh word stirs up anger" (Proverbs 15:1).

If you try to implement this counsel, which is often difficult in the heat of the moment, you will likely see what a dramatic effect it can have upon a difficult conversation. When we feel misunderstood or accused, we can be tempted to reply with a "harsh word," but this will be like pouring fuel on a fire. At this point, if we are slow to speak, we can gain time to recover our senses. A phrase that often defuses difficult situations is: "I'm sorry" (the soft answer), followed by something along the lines of, "Can you explain more about your feelings?" It is hard to go wrong with any "soft answer," particularly when genuinely trying to understand the other person. St. Paul provides further instruction about dealing with anger, quoting from Psalm 4:4 of the danger of sinning in our anger—"Be angry and do not sin" (Ephesians 4:26). He then gives important practical advice, which should be noted by all and especially husbands and wives: "... do not let the sun go down on your anger" (Ephesians 4:26 NASB).

When our spouse or loved one hurts us or causes us to become angry, the normal response (if we can hold our tongue) is to punish them by silence and withdrawal. If we let this period drag on, it can become increasingly difficult to reconcile, and in some extreme situations, husbands and wives have not spoken for years. God's solution is simple—apologize before the sun goes down. Even if you believe the other person is entirely at fault, you need to make the first move, and after reflecting on what you have said or done, say you are sorry for what happened. This, of course, needs to be genuine, but in a conflict, there is always something for which we can be sorry.

In most cases, this will lead to reconciliation, particularly if you are prepared to ask some questions and genuinely seek to understand. You should never be quick to try to be understood, as this can further inflame a difficult situation. If you would like to be heard, it is better to delay presenting your side of the case until the other person feels they have been fully heard.

## The Danger of Offense

All of us have taken offense at various times in our lives. Not only do we become offended by something another person has said or done, but we can become offended by complete strangers (e.g., politicians). Offense implies something that "outrages the moral or physical senses,"[41] and the Book of Proverbs tells us that "A brother offended is harder to be won than a strong city" (Proverbs

---

41  https://www.merriam-webster.com/dictionary/offence

18:19). It is not only necessary not to take offense but also not to give offense. It is less likely that you offend others if you are slow to speak and slow to anger, but sometimes, an offense can be given by something you said or did of which you were unaware.

## The Lure of Triangulation

Unfortunately, our natural inclination is not to seek a resolution in a difficult situation by talking to the person who has offended us. Rather we have a tendency to talk to family members, friends, and co-workers about the issue—in fact, we talk with anyone else but the person involved. Invariably, this leads to further problems as people gossip about what they have heard. Furthermore, we can become even more offended as we tell our story (usually strongly biased toward our viewpoint). This is called triangulation.

Jesus, the Wonderful Counsellor, is the ultimate relationship expert and provides clear advice about how to deal with a relationship problem involving offense, as set out in Matthew 18.

Immediately after recounting a parable about the lost sheep and leaving the ninety-nine sheep to search for the lost one, Jesus gives the following teaching: "… if your brother sins against you, go and tell him his fault between you and him alone. If he hears you, you have gained your brother. But if he will not hear, take with you one or two more, that by the mouth of two or three witnesses every word may be established" (Matthew 18:15–16).

It is critical but difficult to go to a friend, family member, or colleague and talk to them directly about what they have done that has offended you. The easier road is to go and tell others, but invariably, this is a toxic approach that will worsen the situation and may cause an irretrievable breakdown of the relationship.

When you go directly to the person involved, you often find that there was misunderstanding, and the relationship is restored. If not, and the person will not listen, Jesus' counsel is to take one or two other people with you so that there is an independent viewpoint and a witness. However, if the situation involves your wife, my tip is not to take your mother!

If you are going to approach another person to discuss a difficulty or offense, it is essential to do this privately, face-to-face, and not in a public place. There is a great danger in doing this by email or social media, as not only is miscommunication more likely, but the written communication will probably be widely disseminated. This was borne out by the recent libel case in the UK involving two prominent footballers' wives in the so-called "Wagatha Christie" trial.[42] Comments on social media resulted in offense and a libel trial that cost millions of pounds. How much simpler and cheaper it would have been had the women followed Jesus' advice.

As mentioned in a previous chapter, years ago, I had great advice from a boss who said that when you write an email, write it from the viewpoint that if it ends up on the front page of a national newspaper, you won't feel shame or embarrassment. This simple advice has stopped me from writing many emails that could have caused problems for me and others.

## Love Your Enemy

Walking in the seemingly impossible task of loving your enemy is a more challenging task than simply doing no harm and not taking offense. Yet this is Jesus' admonition to his disciples in his long and detailed teaching called "The Sermon on the Mount" (Matthew

---

42  https://www.bbc.com/news/entertainment-arts-61719250

5–7). In this teaching, Jesus compared current acceptable behavior according to the Old Testament with the new higher standard of righteousness (blamelessness) of body, mind, and soul that He was inaugurating. In Matthew 5:43–45, He declares:

"You have heard that it was said, 'You shall love your neighbor and hate your enemy.' But I say to you, love your enemies, bless those who curse you, do good to those who hate you, and pray for those who spitefully use you and persecute you, that you may be sons of your Father in heaven."

This new "law" of a higher standard from another realm has confronted His followers for the last 2,000 years. Loving your enemies is not easy and is only possible by the power of the life of God in us. To make a start, pray for your enemy, then seek to bless and do good to them. Who knows what God may do!

## The Power of Forgiveness

In situations of conflict, especially that which is severe and damaging, forgiveness is the key to healthy continuing relationships and ongoing peace and well-being. Forgiveness is a central theme of Jesus' teaching. Even when nailed to the cross, He asked His Father to forgive those who had nailed Him there to die. Forgiveness must have been an ongoing subject in his private discussions with His disciples. At some stage, Peter asks a question about forgiveness and reading between the lines; it seems as though he had grasped the critical importance of what Jesus was teaching because he asks Jesus this question: "Lord, how often shall my brother sin against me, and I forgive him? Up to seven times?" (Matthew 18:21).

Jesus answers, "*I do not say to you, up to seven times, but up to seventy times seven.*" You don't need to be a top mathematician to calculate that this is a large number of times that we need to forgive someone! Jesus then goes on to tell a parable known as "The Unforgiving Servant" (Matthew 18:21–35). The parable tells the story of a king who is owed an enormous sum of money by one of his servants but out of compassion, the king forgives the debt, for indeed, it was so outstanding that it was impossible to repay. Later, however, this same servant did not show similar compassion towards a fellow servant who owed him a much smaller debt. The king then became angry with the first servant, and Jesus says that the king,

*"... delivered him (*the first servant who owed the incredible amount of money to the king) *to the **torturers** until he should pay all that was due to him. So My heavenly Father **also will do to you** if each of you, from his heart, does not forgive his brother his trespasses"* (Matthew 18:34–35).

The critical point here is that unforgiveness results in you being delivered to the torturers, which is a great incentive for each of us to forgive those whom we feel have wronged us. The Greek word translated as torturer is *basanistēs,* and it means tormentor or torturer, one who finds the truth by use of the rack! It looks bad to be like the unforgiving servant because we all need forgiveness ourselves and don't want to be handed over to the torturers. This group is not well known for their compassion and mercy (I don't think that anyone with these traits gets the job), and so Jesus is telling us that if we fail to forgive others, we are setting ourselves up for severe personal suffering. At this stage, we need to be betting on self-interest, keeping short accounts, and forgiving those close to use (those far away, and anyone else for that matter) so that God doesn't call in our much more considerable debt to Him and we find ourselves in the hands of merciless inquisitors.

I have noticed that in working with groups, in families, amongst friends, and in various work and social situations, causing offense is easy and can result in relationship breakdown. Almost every family has family members who don't speak to each other. In church groups, relationship breakdown and offense have resulted in church splits. In social groups, an action or comment can destroy the harmony and unity of a group. We have a choice: to harbor the pain and resentment and hold onto it like a treasured possession, in which case we will be handed over to the torturers, or we can forgive. I'm sure these torturers are quite real in the spiritual realm, but in any case, I know that I have experienced torture of the soul when I have held on to unforgiveness. This quote from Dr. Lewis Smedes, a professor at Fuller Seminary in California, captures this well: *"To forgive is to set a prisoner free and discover that the prisoner was you."*[43]

When there are marriage disputes, a husband has a vital role as head of the family and the one who is called on to lay down his life (Ephesians 5:25) to be the first to seek reconciliation. This requires humility and being willing to be the first to forgive. I have seen the power of this in my own marriage. However, it is never easy because most husbands have a sense that they are always right!

Why is it so difficult to forgive? There is no simple answer to this, but we can see that problems started with the first family after Adam and Eve were expelled from Eden. They had two sons, and Cain was jealous of his brother Abel because we are told Abel's offering to God was well-regarded. Still, Cain's offering was of *"no regard or respect"* (Genesis 4:4). The Bible says that God told Cain, *"Sin is crouching at the door. And its desire is for you, but you should rule*

---

43 https://www.inspirationalstories.com/quotes/to-forgive-is-to-set-a-prisoner-of-lewis-b-smedes-quote/

*over it*" (Genesis 4:7). In other words, you have a choice about how you respond to a perceived slight. In the face of anger, Cain chose to kill his brother Abel. This scenario has been played, literally or figuratively, out millions of times over the succeeding millennia. We are potential victims of anger and unforgiveness and their consequences today.

From our ancestors in the Garden, we have a genetic predisposition to hold onto the pain and trauma of offense and find ourselves (mostly unknowingly) handed over to the tormentors or inquisitors. The question then is, how do we forgive? It isn't easy, and all of us can feel justified in harboring resentment and anger toward the one who has wronged us. Forgiveness is only possible by letting go of our pride, humbling ourselves, and releasing the debt we perceive they owe us. This is incredibly difficult because usually, we feel that the other person has done something far worse than we have. Yet, humbling ourselves is the foundation of forgiveness as we understand that our debt before God, for which we have been forgiven, is much greater than any debt that someone owes us as a result of something they have done. The alternative that we need to keep in our minds and that can move us towards an attitude of forgiveness is being handed over to the torturers.

While we need to forgive unconditionally, I add a caveat for the many abuse victims. Forgiving even our abusers is not saying that what they did was not wrong, and in no sense is there a justification for their actions. It doesn't even mean you need to see them and restore the relationship. It does mean that you need to forgive them in your heart, between you and God. This is the only way that you, the prisoner, can be set free.

# KEY POINTS ABOUT WISDOM IN CONFLICT

- **If you are wronged, assume that there was no ill intent**. Offense is often a matter of perception, and we assume malintent because we can't understand why a person said or did something. Most people don't have bad intentions or a desire to deliberately injure us. We can prevent bitterness from taking root in our hearts, assuming that whatever was said or done did not intend to harm us. Unfortunately, we often assign good intent to our actions but bad intent to those of others.

- **Avoid triangulation.** Due to the broken human condition, humans seem to have an inherited flaw, which results in us complaining about someone to everyone apart from the person we feel has wronged us! Jesus' counsel is, *"If your brother sins against you, go and tell him his fault between you and him* **alone**. *If he hears you, you have gained your brother"* (Matthew 18:15). This also is true in a situation where we realize that someone is offended with us (Matthew 5:23–24). Many problems can be prevented by talking to the person who offended us rather than to others.

- **Be swift to hear, slow to speak, and slow to get angry.** This advice from Jesus' half-brother James who wrote this in a letter more than 2,000 years ago, is as important today as it was then.

- **Forgiveness is the key to any conflict and means letting go and releasing the person from the debt that you perceive they owe you**. Something about our need for personal justification results in us holding on to offense. This is not God's way and does not lead to health and well-being. If we

117

remember that unforgiveness results in us *"being handed over to the torturers"* (Matthew 18:34–35), we should be motivated to let go of resentment and unforgiveness.

- **Be prepared to act first in conflict and ask for forgiveness**. This is one of the hardest things to do, and as my old boss said, *"I may not always be right, but I am never wrong."* This is how we all tend to feel. In conflict, it is essential to be prepared to be the first to step in with a gentle word and seek forgiveness for our part in the breakdown. This is particularly important for a husband, as head of the family.

- **Ask God to help us and bring healing from the pain of the offense**. My own experience and the experience of many whom I've talked to is that when we feel mistreated, we don't want to risk being mistreated again. We then often remove ourselves or cut off contact. There may be times when this is appropriate when there has been abuse, but on the other hand, if we do it out of unforgiveness, then that choice hands us over to the torturers. God's ways lead to life. When we forgive someone, we are released from the torment that comes from unforgiveness, and much of the pain from the incident will go. Forgiveness is often the first step on the road to healing. God is a God who desires to draw near, and when we ask Him for help, He gives it. He knows how to bring healing to our hearts; if we ask Him, He will bring us wisdom to deal with relationship difficulties.

We have examined some of the critical issues of wisdom in friendship, communication, and conflict, and the next important area to consider is the area of planning. Planning is vital because, as the old saying goes, "Without a plan, you are just wandering about." However, plans can themselves be constraining, so planning needs great care.

# CHAPTER 8
# WISDOM IN PLANNING

*"Plans fail for lack of counsel, but with many advisors, they succeed." (Proverbs 15:22 NIV)*

In the Book of Ecclesiastes, King Solomon provides a critical perspective on life that is as true today as 3,000 years ago. Solomon wrote (Ecclesiastes 3:1):

"To everything there is a season,

A time for every purpose under heaven."

Solomon speaks of the importance of understanding the season you are in and not trying to fight against the natural order. The subsequent verses amplify this central idea with examples of the times and seasons in a person's life and the importance of recognizing which season we are in. There are times for weeping and laughing, mourning and dancing, silence and speaking, love and hate, and war and peace, amongst many others (see more detail in Chapter 16). Solomon outlines what is potentially one of the most important ideas about planning because without understanding the season we are in, bad decisions can be made. Without awareness of the constraints and opportunities and weighing all the elements in the balance, any plans you try to make will likely fail. Before starting any project, you need to understand the season you are in and whether this is the time frame for such an event. Is it the season for marriage, building, risk-taking, rest and reflection, planting, healing, a job change, or consolidation?

## Planning and God's Plans

In the period before the Great Flood, Noah (in contrast to others of his generation) "walked with God" (Genesis 6:9). This closeness to the Creator also is emphasized by Jesus, who described it this way to His disciples:

"I am the vine, you are the branches. He who abides in Me, and I in him, bears much fruit; **for without Me you can do nothing**" (John 15:5).

Of course, we can do many things, but it is clear that if our plans are not aligned with God's plans, they will profit us little and come to nothing. The key is to grow in "walking with God," which isn't easy in the rush of daily life, the intrusion of social media, and an invisible God who, left to our own devices, we can ignore. We can conceive many plans, but they have no eternal value unless the plans align with those of God. In Proverbs 16:3, King Solomon says, "Commit your works to the LORD, And your thoughts will be established." We need to commit what we do to God, and He says He will bring to us and establish the thoughts and ideas we need. His concept seems inverted to human wisdom, but it is God's wisdom.

The fear of the Lord provides the context for us in the big picture of planning because if our plans are in opposition to His plans and His law, then they will surely fail or at least fail to have a life-giving impact. There is a mystery in God's counsel in Proverbs 16:3 concerning committing our work to Him. If we learn to walk with God and commit our work (and daily life to Him), we will learn to hear His voice, and our ideas and direction will be clear. In a practical sense, we need to establish times to be with God, just as with our friends, and prayer is simply a conversation with God. Of course, rather than just speaking all the time, we need to leave room for God to speak. It is extraordinary that as we read His word in the Bible, God often will speak to us about a particular matter in our own hearts. He can also speak through a dream, a vision, another person, a thought or picture, or sometimes just a sense in our hearts of the right way to go. It is important to remember that all of God's ways are peace (1 Corinthians 14:33). If we feel anxious about a particular decision or direction, it is likely the wrong decision. God will confirm His way with a sense of peace, even in the most challenging circumstances.

The "fear of the Lord" and acknowledging our dependence on Him provides us with a framework in planning, knowing that this is God's world and we need to understand His ways (which the Bible tells us are not our ways—Isaiah 55:8–10). It is worthwhile then examining some accounts in the Bible where God has provided a plan to His people and examining the principles involved. Let's look at the plan God gave Noah before the Great Flood.

## God Gives Noah a Plan

In the days of Noah, the violence and corruption were terrible, and God said of humanity that "every intent of the thoughts of his heart was only evil continually" (Genesis 6:5). God's plan was radical—to essentially wipe humanity and all of the creatures from the face of the earth.

The Bible tells us that God gave precise directions to Noah (Genesis 6:14–16):

"Make yourself an ark of gopherwood; make rooms in the ark, and cover it inside and outside with pitch. And this is how you shall make it: The length of the ark shall be three hundred cubits, its width fifty cubits, and its height thirty cubits. You shall make a window for the ark, and you shall finish it to a cubit from above; and set the door of the ark in its side. You shall make it with lower, second, and third decks."

This was a major project; Noah's sons presumably helped him as he toiled away to build this massive ark. [It is interesting that the word translated as "ark" comes from the Hebrew word תֵּבָה (têḇâ), which is used in only one other place in the Bible—to describe the reed basket that Moses was placed in when his mother set him adrift on the Nile (Exodus 2:3). In both the cases of Noah and Moses, those in the vessel were kept safe through the providence of God who brought about a rescue through the water.] Noah believed God concerning the coming flood, although the project must have seemed like complete folly to the rest of those on the earth. This was, of course, until the first rains started to fall (notably, it had never rained before, but water rose up from the ground), and the waters rose over 40 days and nights of continuous rain. Noah and his family were saved by his obedience to God's directions because he was his generation's only righteous (blameless) and law-abiding person. God's righteousness is not the same as ours, and our society seems to move increasingly away from God's ways to those in opposition to God.

In Noah's situation, his obedience provided a fresh beginning for humanity. In everything we plan or do, large or small, it is important to "seek the Lord" to ensure that our plans aren't in opposition to God's plans but are aligned with Him as He establishes our thoughts and our steps (Proverbs 16:9). To have God's blessing, our plans need to pursue that which is righteous (morally upright) and to shun evil. As with Noah, we need to be aware of the times and seasons to understand what God is doing and to ensure that we are aligned with His plans. God revealed to Noah that the earth was coming into a time of judgment and established Noah's thoughts concerning the building of an ark. This enabled Noah, his family, and many creatures to come through this terrible season of judgment.

The story of Noah contrasts sharply with the story of the Tower of Babel outlined in Genesis Chapter 11. After the flood, as the earth was repopulated, there was only one language, and those on the earth developed a cunning plan in the plains of Shinar. The Bible tells us they decided: "Let us make a name for ourselves, lest we be scattered abroad over the face of the whole earth" (Genesis 11:4).

These plans, possibly implemented to beat any future flood, were in opposition to God's ways as men sought to make "a name" (in Hebrew - שֵׁם šêm), which carries the sense of a position, authority, and honor. In other words, men wanted to establish themselves as the authority over the earth. To do this, they planned to build a city with "a tower whose top is in the heavens" (Genesis 11:4). So soon after the judgment of the flood, people sought to elevate themselves to a similar status to God. The Bible tells us that God saw that with unity of purpose and language, anything could be achieved, as men sought to emulate God. So "The LORD scattered them abroad from there over the face of all the earth, and they ceased building the city. Therefore its name is called Babel because there the LORD confused the language of all the earth; and from there, the LORD scattered them abroad over the face of all the earth" (Genesis 11:8–9).

God did not tolerate men's plans as they sought to make themselves His equal. These plans of long ago are not dissimilar in intent to modern transhumanist ideas to alter DNA and create a fusion of man and machine, which they say will enhance human capabilities and even secure eternal life. Indeed, God looks upon these plans with anger like He did thousands of years ago in the Plains of Shinar.

It is important to note here that the Bible does tell us that in the times of the end, the plans of humanity for evil on the earth will be so great that God will come with judgment to cleanse the earth of evil. The stories of Noah and Babel are instructive in the big picture of planning today. Sometimes, God calls on us to do something that doesn't make sense and looks impossible. Nonetheless, if it is God's plan, the project will prosper. In contrast, failure is inevitable if our plan involves a project against the foundation of God's law and seeks to elevate ourselves to the same status as God.

## Dangers in Planning

Planning always carries the danger of hubris—a sense that we are all powerful and knowledgeable enough to implement successful strategies even when all the variables, notably those related to human behavior, are difficult to predict. The Book of Proverbs tells us (Proverbs 15:22), "Without consultation, plans are frustrated, but with many counselors, they succeed" (NASB). Many plans fail because people attempt to implement a plan designed by just a few without adequate consideration of some factors that could jettison the project. God's wisdom from King Solomon advises that a plan will more likely be successful if more advisors are brought into the planning process. This will potentially bring combined wisdom to bear, allowing more ideas but also identifying more potential points of failure. It also is essential to include people who are hostile towards the plan because you may well have overlooked some critical flaw.

The idea of a five-year plan became popularized by Stalin and his accomplices in the Soviet Union in 1928.[44] The concept directly challenged capitalism and its reliance on the marketplace. Stalin focused on building an industrial Soviet Union and achieving state control of agriculture. Despite the plan leading to extreme food shortages and the deaths of millions, Stalin pressed on with another four such plans. This era of Soviet planning is acknowledged as one that brought extensive turmoil and death. Those in charge were required to deliver the unrealistic outcomes demanded by Stalin and his inner circle, and there were no incentives for people apart from not being shot. The Soviet style of planning demonstrated some of the inherent dangers of planning:

- Inflexibility—the need to achieve the projected results, no matter the constraints and the unanticipated adverse effects;

- Lack of incentives for people to work hard when there is no reward;

- The likelihood of ignoring other possibilities and opportunities as people become single-minded to achieve the dictates of the plan;

- Unrealistic expectations—plans are almost always optimistic, and so many plans end up in failure;

- Lack of understanding of constraints and particularly the people factor. Most organizational restructuring plans are implemented with little consideration of the impacts on people; because of this, there often is significant resistance to the plan.

---

44  https://www.historyhit.com/first-five-year-plan-begins/

Despite the dangers of planning and a poor track record of scarcely any successful government plans, there still seems to be an attraction in most bureaucracies to produce glossy five-year plans that are hundreds of pages long and impossible to understand.

I have worked with many groups to develop such plans, and they are helpful if the plans are loosely held and are used to chart a broad direction. Plans work most effectively when some primary goals are identified and agreed upon, allowing individuals to direct their efforts. A one-page plan briefly outlining the primary goals and responsibilities is an excellent and straightforward format enabling regular review. Some groups assist in this process, such as the One Page Business Plan Company,[45] and there are several resources on the internet, such as this reference (see footnote), about how to write a one-page business plan.[46]

## Personal Planning

I have been involved in personal planning since I joined a group of CEOs (The Executive Connection)[47] more than 20 years ago. One of the major benefits for me was a planning process each year that began with the question of purpose—who am I, and what contribution do I want to make? Each group member then worked on a range of personal goals (health, family, vacations, relationships, spiritual) and business goals (business growth, new markets, new products, finances) and shared them with the group. The process was helpful as it required reflection on the previous year and what had gone either well or badly. Here are some of the critical questions that can help develop a personal plan:

---

45  https://onepagebusinessplan.com/
46  https://articles.bplans.com/how-to-write-a-business-plan-on-just-one-page/
47  https://tec.com.au/

1. **What are the most important goals, which, if achieved in the year ahead, would provide a sense of satisfaction?** My experience in planning was that I set too many goals, and as the year proceeded, I lost track of the things that I thought were most important. I found it valuable to determine (from all the ideas I had) what goals would have the most impact on my life and the lives of those closest to me. This takes quite a lot of effort to work through various goals to find the one that will have the most impact on your life and those around you.

2. **What are the specific projects that will make the most impact?** The more detailed the idea associated with a goal, the more likely you are to achieve it. This is because you have had to think carefully about what it is that will provide the outcome that will have the most significant impact. For example, rather than lose weight, you can make the weight loss specific (e.g., 10 lbs) and by a certain date, with weekly milestones to assess progress. Most of us will be drawn towards goals that we know we can achieve, but it is worthwhile considering those that you know would have a significant impact on your life but you are avoiding.

3. **Who are the most important people you are seeking to impact, and how do you need them involved?** None of us lives or works in isolation. Your plans will always include and impact other people, so it is good to consult them (Proverbs 15:22 tells us that plans succeed with many advisors). You can obtain ideas and feedback, and those closest to you can help keep you accountable.

4. **What resources (finance, people, equipment, time, etc.) will be needed?** Apart from finance required to achieve a

goal such as travel, time is probably the resource that is scarcest for most people. Most of us use our time poorly, and social media is a constant distraction. Setting time aside in your calendar to work on and assess progress with your goals is critical, as well as identifying the major areas in your life where time is wasted. It is extremely difficult to be sufficiently self-disciplined to change long-term habits without a major effort to reorient your life and priorities.

5. **How will you know if you are successful?** The old management edict says, "If you can't measure it, you can't manage it." Implementing methods for measuring your progress is essential at the start of a plan. For example, in writing this book, I started with the goal of writing a book on wisdom this year, which was specific but a challenge without much definition. As I thought about it further, I realized that I needed to work out a timeline for each component of the process. When I examined the whole writing process, I realized I needed to break the project into bite-sized pieces. To complete the book in 12 months, I needed to finish the initial writing in three to four months, which translated into a goal of writing a chapter (about 3,000 to 4,000 words) each week. Then revision, editing, etc., would take another two to three months, with a final product being ready for printing after eight to nine months. Breaking the process down and setting clear shorter-term goals allowed me to suddenly make significant progress, whereas the larger goal remained an unrealizable dream.

6. **What are the most critical risks to be considered?** My experience is that risk is either underestimated or overestimated. Nonetheless, in most goal setting, risk should be

determined and evaluated. The significant risk to most personal goals is not making a start. The old saying that the most challenging part of any project is making a start is true. The other significant risk is that a project is crowded out by apparently more urgent tasks or just time-wasting.

7. **What are the relationships you want to focus on in your personal plan?** Relationships are complex and invariably tricky. It is impossible to be responsible for someone else, but focusing time and love on relationships you sense need nurturing is possible. The key is understanding the person and what they value. For example, it is no use buying gifts if what they love is time with you. Most of us don't put enough effort into our relationships, particularly those with our spouses. Men, in particular, have a tendency to take their wives for granted, and data show that most men are surprised when their wives leave them. Prioritizing time for critical relationships is the most crucial part of any personal plan.

8. **How will you review and make adjustments to your plan?** In the early years of personal planning, I felt exhilarated after completing my plan for the year, which I often placed on the refrigerator to keep the plan in view. However, it wasn't long before the plan became obscured by children's drawings, and I failed to notice it anymore. It is essential to schedule regular reviews of your plan in your calendar so that you can make adjustments and monitor your progress.

9. **What is my aim regarding work-life balance?** This has become a significant concern for young people today and is definitely a question worth addressing in your plan. It

comes back to the idea of times and seasons. There are times in careers when long hours must be committed to work, but if this is the case, this season must be limited. It is easier than we think to become a workaholic and find ourselves in a place where our relationships with family have been irrevocably damaged. It is vital to review work-life balance regularly to determine if there are signs of stress or difficulty in yourself or those around you. If your work has become overly dominating in your life, the signs of stress for you and your family usually are evident, but it can be easy to ignore warning signals. I once heard about a "bank of relationships" where you can intentionally make "deposits" by spending time and energy with those closest to you. At some stage, when there is a crisis, these "deposits" can be withdrawn, but you can suddenly find that the account is empty and you are "overdrawn." By this stage, the relationship usually is destroyed. It is important not to run down our funds in the bank of relationships.

10. **Who can provide support and accountability?** Once you have completed a personal plan, one of the most important things you can do is to find a trusted friend or family member to review your progress regularly. I have found that a quarterly review is helpful, and how quickly three months go by is remarkable. Having a friend review your plan and ask questions about your progress is helpful in personal accountability. This process has kept me on track when I have forgotten about some critical elements of my goals.

# KEY POINTS ABOUT WISDOM IN PLANNING

- It is essential to understand the season you are in and, from this understanding, orient your priorities.

- Your plans must align with God's priorities and purposes, and it is crucial to seek God and learn to "walk with Him" to determine if your priorities align with God's. An important way of knowing this is whether what you are doing is accompanied by a sense of peace rather than anxiety.

- God often calls us to do something impossible. We need to recognize if God is calling us to do something to not deviate from the plan, even if it looks ridiculous to others.

- Plans fail for lack of consultation, but with many advisors, they succeed (Proverbs 15:22). It is good to consult widely and essential to include those who have reservations about the plan as well as those who agree with you.

- Plans invariably involve people, so it is essential to consider how the plan will impact others e.g travel, working hours, location etc.

- The best plans have been refined to just a few goals, including only those that will have the most impact.

- Prioritization of relationships often is forgotten in planning. Failure to plan to invest in our most important relationships can often result in relationship breakdown and its consequences.

Planning almost invariably involves some form of further education, either in formal or informal ways. In the next chapter, we will examine the area of education and the opportunities and challenges associated with what is increasingly becoming a tool of state indoctrination.

# CHAPTER 9
# WISDOM IN EDUCATION

*"You shall teach them diligently to your children, and shall talk of them when you sit in your house, when you walk by the way when you lie down, and when you rise up."*
*(Deuteronomy 6:7)*

I will never forget my first day at veterinary school. The Dean of the Faculty spoke to us bright-eyed young students ready for our first day and the excitement about becoming veterinarians. He said: "Look to your right, then look to your left. One of you won't be here next year."

This was terrifying but accurate because around one-third of the class had failed the course at the end of that first year. It was a harsh dose of reality after high school, but it was actually tough love—or perhaps just tough! His statement certainly had a profound impact on me, and I thought to myself, "I don't want to be one of the 33% who fails," so each night, I worked hard to learn the lessons of the day's lectures and practical classes.

In my career, I went on to teach at universities in Australia and other countries and saw a gradual change in teaching and assessment approaches. Over time, more challenging subjects were made easier by simplifying assessment tasks. The idea of "student-centered learning" suddenly became a mantra for lecturers, and feedback was gathered to determine how each of the courses was regarded by the students. Fewer students failed, and eventually, over time, almost all students passed through the system. Special consideration was given to some students with various forms of intellectual and emotional challenges, and it seemed as though the main task of professors was to please students rather than to teach and uphold the educational standards necessary to ensure students achieved the required level of knowledge to perform professionally.

There is much sense in making education user-friendly, encouraging, and considerate of the views of students. Still, I have a nagging feeling that the old ways, where standards were upheld, and a student either met them or failed, was the way of wisdom. Grade inflation has occurred in most educational institutions today, and an educational culture has developed where every student gets a prize, and every student is a winner. Upon graduation, young graduates get mugged by the reality of life and an unforgiving and pressured work environment for which they are unprepared. Education also has become infused with supposed "social justice" measures such as equity and environmental politics. In most countries, standards of literacy and numeracy have radically fallen, even in the face of massive increases in spending on education by governments. The reality is that modern education is not producing capable, independent, and critical thinkers. The time is long overdue to return to the ancient ways.

In this chapter, we will examine some of the ancient foundations of learning and the benefits and hazards of modern approaches to education.

# Ancient Paths of Education

The introductory verses of the Book of Proverbs are an excellent summary of the mission of education. King Solomon writes that his proverbs are designed to teach "wisdom and instruction, to understand words of insight, to receive instruction in wise dealing, in righteousness, justice and equity; to give prudence to the simple, knowledge and discretion to the youth" (Proverbs 1:2–5 ESV).

Unfortunately, our tendency across time and civilizations has been to consider ourselves "wise in our own eyes" (Proverbs 3:7) and to think that we are more intelligent and more insightful than previous generations. In another collection of King Solomon's wisdom, the Book of Ecclesiastes, he says:

"That which has been is what will be,

That which is done is what will be done,

And there is nothing new under the sun.

Is there anything of which it may be said,

'See, this is new?'

It has already been in ancient times before us" (Ecclesiastes 1:9–10).

We may think that we have new ways and new ideas, and of course, it is true that various technologies have brought many benefits. However, in the current age of the internet, biotechnology, nanotechnology, artificial intelligence, and the metaverse, there is "nothing new under the sun" in the fundamentals of human behavior. Self-interest and greed abound, and pride and selfishness derail us in our business and personal lives. We need to return to the basics—God has created a world where everything we need has been provided. We are stewards of God's creation and need to understand God's laws and His ways so that we can prosper.

In the Book of Proverbs, King Solomon proposes an overarching foundation for education:

"The fear of the Lord is the beginning of knowledge, but fools despise wisdom and instruction" (Proverbs 1:7).

This statement is just as true today as it was 3,000 years ago. The fear of the Lord, outlined in the introductory chapters of this book, is the basis of all wisdom. Without fear of God, which is an understanding that there is One who made all things, who designed natural laws into the fabric of creation, and ultimately to whom we are accountable, our learning is fruitless. The Hebrew scribes understood and wrote about the fear of the Lord as they taught God's law in the Torah (the first five books of the Old Testament).

Approaches to education varied greatly in ancient civilizations and were often only available to the elite. However, in most civilizations, education focused on literacy and numeracy, a study of the classics, and all of this in the context of the development of the mind and the ability to think critically. At the heart of all education was a commitment to promoting truth and an understanding of the natural law.

## Modern Education

In more recent times, educators have moved away from objective truth to relative truth, and the post-modernism movement, founded on the idea that there is no such thing as truth, has been influential in all parts of the educational system. State-based curricula emphasize the "progressive" views of the day: climate change, sex education, gender theory, critical race theory, indigenous culture, and other areas that the educators have deemed necessary for a "successful" society. Even subjects like mathematics have been commandeered by the racial equity brigade, and now it is possible that 2 + 2 may not equal four. The responsibility for education has been wrenched away from the family by the State, which, not surprisingly, has an agenda of turning children into "useful" state citizens rather than independent, critical thinkers.

It is widely agreed that the most influential thinker related to modern education was the Columbia University academic Dr. John Dewey. Dewey was a secular socialist who radically transformed the face of educational theory in the U.S. during the 1930s and 1940s. While Dewey died in 1952, his influence lives on in Western education today, and during his life, he was president of both the American Philosophical Association and the American Psychological Association.[48] Dewey wanted to see a secular underpinning of education, and he wrote:[49] "There is no god and there is no soul. Hence, there is no need for the props of traditional religion. With dogma and creed excluded, then immutable truth is dead and buried. There is no room for fixed and natural law or permanent moral absolutes." Dewey's whole agenda was to undermine the Christian foundations of the U.S. and to replace objective truth with relativism. He was one of the first signatories of "The Humanist Manifesto,"[50] which not only promoted the non-existence of God but endorsed socialism and communism.

Dewey was influential in transforming U.S. and Western education into the progressive, social relativist, humanist philosophy that we

---

48  https://wysu.org/content/commentary/john-dewey-religion
49  https://illinoisfamily.org/education/john-deweys-public-schools-re-placed-christianity-with-collectivist-humanism/
50  https://americanhumanist.org/what-is-humanism/manifesto1/

find in all Western nations today. At the heart of Dewey's assault on the foundations of the U.S. was his undermining of the concept of God-given "unalienable rights," as set out in the Declaration of Independence. If there is no God, there are no "unalienable rights." This secular, anti-God, relativist philosophy has been widely disseminated in all areas of education, is the foundation of Western curricula, and is supported by teachers and professors. It's not surprising that the end result is a humanistic, secular, and socialist ideology among young people. The results are the promotion of "progressive" ideas such as gender fluidity, critical race theory, etc., because education is founded on relativism and rejection of the concept of absolute truth. In education, it is time to get back to basics and the wisdom of the ancients.

## Ancient Hebrew Education

The Torah provided the foundation for learning for Jewish children, and they were taught to learn extensive passages of Scripture by heart. At the time the children of Israel were about to be led out of the desert and into the Promised Land, across the River Jordan, God proclaimed to Joshua the centrality of the Books of the Law to the nation: "This Book of the Law shall not depart from your mouth, but you shall meditate in it day and night, that you may observe to do according to all that is written in it. For then you will make your way prosperous, and then you will have good success" (Joshua 1:8).

God made it clear that meditating in His book was the critical factor for success in the new land they were entering. The Hebrew word for meditate is הָגָה, transliterated as hâgâ. This word doesn't mean to think and reflect on something, but rather, it means to recite or mutter or even to growl or moan. To meditate is definitely an active process where you mutter or even sing the verses "day and night." It is interesting that in the time of the New Testament, Paul suggests something similar when he writes, "Faith comes by hearing and hearing by the word of God" (Romans 10:17). Speaking the word of God out loud such that we hear it, sets us up to grow in faith.

In Hebrew education, there was a strong awareness of the need to raise children in the "fear of the Lord" and to avoid the polytheistic cultures around them. A Talmudic story about two rabbis helps us understand this point:

"... In the Talmud, there is a story of a progressive young Rabbi who wished to study Greek on the grounds that he had mastered the Law. An older Rabbi reminded him of the words of Joshua: 'This book of the Law shall not depart out of thy mouth; but thou shall meditate therein day and night.' 'Go then and consider,' he said, 'which is the hour which is neither of the day or of the night, and in it thou mayest study Greek wisdom.'"[51]

The Jews are called the "People of the Book" because the Tanakh (or what in Christian traditions is called the Old Testament) was the basis for transmitting the essence of spiritual life, philosophy, culture, and language from generation to generation. Teaching children was done by the teacher reciting a passage of the Torah, after which the class would repeat it. This was done until the passage had been memorized, and so a critical part of learning involved long sessions of listening to the teacher, followed by class repetition. Such ideas have been largely lost and replaced by the modern notion of the "teacher as a facilitator," who may not have specific knowledge in any given area.

---

51  https://worldhistory.us/ancient-history/ancient-jewish-education-of-children-and-use-of-scripture.php

Similarly, in the early days of the American colonies and even after independence, the Bible provided the foundation for education, which included education in morals. This is undoubtedly why John Adams, one of the U.S. Founding Fathers, said: "Our constitution was made only for a moral and religious people. It is wholly inadequate to the government of any other."[52]

Modern education has moved a long way from the days of solid and sound education methods that have withstood the passage of time. It is worthwhile examining the approach to education outlined in the Old Testament (Tanakh). This was an education in the home, under the responsibility of parents, using the Bible as the basis for learning. Not only was this the foundation for Jewish education but also for later Western civilization.

## Educational Lessons From the Bible

Across most of the West, parents have handed over their educational responsibilities to the state. Regarding the family, this approach needs to be revised as teachers often promote values that are opposed to those of many parents. Some of the earliest accounts detailing the importance of parents taking responsibility for their children's learning occurred when Moses led Israel in the desert around Mount Sinai. After outlining the Ten Commandments, Moses provides instruction that is still relevant today:

"Hear, O Israel: The LORD our God, the LORD is one! You shall love the LORD your God with all your heart, with all your soul, and with all your strength.

---

52 https://constitutionallaw.regent.edu/preserving-a-constitution-designed-for-a-moral-and-religious-people/

"And these words which I command you today shall be in your heart. You shall teach them diligently to your children, and shall talk of them when you sit in your house, when you walk by the way, when you lie down, and when you rise up. You shall bind them as a sign on your hand, and they shall be as frontlets between your eyes. You shall write them on the doorposts of your house and on your gates." (Deuteronomy 6:4–9)

These verses have been spoken by succeeding generations of Jews for 3,500 years. Significantly, these instructions start with the imperative form of the verb to hear (in Hebrew שְׁמַע transliterated as šâma', meaning "hear"!). In Hebrew, this word carries the idea of hearing diligently and obeying rather than just passively listening. Moses' instruction is that God is to be central to everything in life and that loving God with all your heart, all your soul, and all your strength is the fundamental purpose of life, out of which all other goals are born. Jesus later reiterated this desert commandment (Matthew 22:37) as the most important instruction in God's law.

Moses' admonition to parents was to teach the law of God, which had been embedded in their own hearts by recitation to their children. The words of God are to be part of the household's daily life from morning to evening. There were no special teaching times for children but an infusion of God and His ways into the day in all the activities of family life. Moses also indicates that writing critical parts of God's law in various visible locations in the house is important in fostering learning and obedience. Such a visual display is essential for modern households today. This is very different from the contemporary concept of removing children from family life to "educate" them with curricula that have no oversight from parents and, in many cases, seek to alienate children from parents.

King Solomon confirms this basic commandment by reiterating the roles of the mother and father in teaching their children.

- "My son, hear the instruction of your father,

  And do not forsake the law of your mother" (Proverbs 1:8).

- "Hear, my children, the instruction of a father,

  And give attention to know understanding;
  For I give you good doctrine:
  Do not forsake my law" (Proverbs 4:1–2).

- "Train up a child in the way he should go,

  And when he is old he will not depart from it" (Proverbs 22:6).

The significance of the truth captured in the latter Proverb has been recognized by groups like the Jesuits and the communists in the Soviet Union, under Vladimir Lenin, as a strategy to gain access to and influence young minors. It is true that if parents don't provide an influential role in nurturing and forming the thinking of their children, schools, universities, social media, and entertainment organizations will do the job for them, with the disastrous results seen today.

Most parents, who are Christian or even sympathetic towards Christianity and its teachings, are unaware that the whole of the education system has become anti-Christian and anti-God. All school curricula have a secular humanist, post-modern philosophy, and it can become almost impossible for parents to combat the culture and values of their children's teachers and peers. This is why home schooling, with its origins in the Bible and in the natural order, should be carefully considered by parents. Home schooling allows parents to influence the nurture and development of their children's character, values, and learning.

# Home Schooling

The season of childhood is a critical time for the encouragement and development of the unique talents and gifts of each child, but parents' time and availability are at a premium. Children also need to learn boundaries, responsibility, and the importance of hard work, amongst many other things. The school system is no longer trustworthy, and many parents have recognized this, as can be seen from the increasing numbers who are home schooling their children. It is wise for parents to understand that this season of childhood is brief, and it is critical to invest the time and effort needed to build a strong relationship with the child. Television, social media, and video games are convenient ways to entertain children but are poor alternatives to individual attention.

Home schooling was the original form of education and was the only educational form available in the early days of the U.S. colonies. The tradition of home schooling has continued in the U.S. but is rare in many other countries and even illegal in some European states. The latest data indicates that there are 3.7 million home-schooled children in the U.S. and that North Carolina, Florida, and Georgia are the states with the most home schoolers.[53] Home schoolers outperform institutionally educated children in national examinations.[54] Home schooling is growing rapidly, and data from the last five years indicate a 10% per annum compounding growth rate. Undoubtedly, this is related to concerns that parents have about the indoctrination of their children with the latest "progressive" ideas.

53  https://parentingmode.com/homeschooling/
54  https://modernhomeschoolfamily.com/2017/04/20/what-the-research-says-about-homeschooling/

Home schooling provides the following advantages:

- Designing a curriculum that is individualized and can help identify and develop a child's strengths and assist them in weaker areas;

- Flexibility in a timetable and the ability to use the time that otherwise would be wasted in various unproductive school activities;

- Prevention of bullying and harassment;

- Opportunity to nurture religious and moral values that are important to the family;

- Fostering the relationship between parents and children;

- Reinforcing the role of parents in the education of their children.

I have noticed a proliferation of resources for home schooling on the internet, and parents need no longer feel that they are wandering about in the dark without support. Home schooling does involve sacrifice, as at least one parent needs to be home to supervise the children's education. Many people think that there is a problem in the socialization of home-schooled children, but my experience in meeting many home-schooled children does not indicate that this is an issue. It is undoubtedly true that most home schoolers don't spend all their free time on social media, but this is a major advantage in today's society.

There can be some challenges in the transition to college because, at least in some countries, a state-issued high school diploma is not available for home schoolers. However, my experience is that there are many pathways for home schoolers to make this transition. Furthermore, home-schooled children are innovative and capable of determining how to meet entrance requirements for higher education. However, it does raise the issue of how important it is that children receive a college education.

# College/Higher Education

Fifty years ago, college education was completed by less than 10% of the population in most Western countries, but today, this percentage has increased to more than 50%.[55] You may think these figures might be the cause for celebration, but having been actively involved in college education for 50 years, I would not recommend college education for most today. A possible exception is those wanting to pursue the hard sciences and professions, where a qualification is needed for entry. The "progressive" educators have purloined every sector of higher education, and now college education is little more than an indoctrination by the left-wing thought police. There was a time when education taught critical thinking and was designed to expose students to a wide range of thoughts and opinions. However, today educators are under pressure just to provide one view that fits current "progressive" ideologies, and students are given "trigger warnings" (areas of study where they may feel uncomfortable or traumatized) if required to read many of the literary classics. The cost of college education also has become prohibitive, and students can graduate with a debt of several hundreds of thousands of dollars. Not only that, but they graduate having been brainwashed with a left-wing ideology.

If a high school student has aptitude and interest, it would be more beneficial to enter vocational training where fundamental practical skills are learned. Today, education at all levels has

---

55  https://www.census.gov/data/tables/2000/dec/phc-t-41.html

become mostly indoctrination, and alternative pathways with more traditional teaching methods are needed to help raise and educate a new generation of critical thinkers who are literate in the foundations of Western civilization.

## KEY POINTS ABOUT WISDOM IN EDUCATION

- There is "nothing new under the sun," and when considering modern education, it is important to study the ideas and methods of education in ancient times.

- "The fear of the Lord is the beginning of knowledge, but fools despise wisdom and instruction" (Proverbs 1:7). Therefore, no factual basis for understanding ourselves and the world around us can be built without this foundation.

- Under the influence of the "progressive" 1930s educator John Dewey, modern education has promoted an atheistic, humanistic philosophy where there are no foundational truths.

- Education of the children of Israel in ancient times involved learning extensive passages of the Old Testament by heart as the foundation for understanding the world, good and evil, one's self, relationships, work, etc.

- Moses taught that God's instructions were central to family life. He wrote that "you shall teach them diligently to your children, and shall talk of them when you sit in your house, when you walk by the way, when you lie down, and when you rise up" (Deuteronomy 6:7).

- According to ancient biblical wisdom, parents need to be actively involved in the education of their children, and King

Solomon wrote that children needed to heed the direction of their parents, "My son, hear the instruction of your father,

- And do not forsake the law of your mother" (Proverbs 1:8).

- Home schooling is the ancient original means of educating children and provides the best alternative to the modern educational system, designed to undermine parents' authority and influence. The percentage of parents home schooling their children is increasing significantly in the U.S. There are many online resources to assist parents.

- A college education is an increasingly expensive form of left-wing indoctrination. It is more beneficial if the high school student has the aptitude and interest to enter vocational training where fundamental practical skills are learned.

From here, let's move on from wisdom in education to wisdom in work and explore some of the ancient wisdom related to work.

# CHAPTER 10
# WISDOM IN WORK

*"The Lord God took the man and put him in the garden of Eden to work it and keep it." (Genesis 2:15)*

I have had the privilege to encourage and counsel many young (and even older) people at critical times in their life journeys to help them to think about their future careers and discover the best future work or career options. I have found no better advice about future careers and work than this quote from Howard Thurman. Thurman was a 20th-century theologian and philosopher, the grandson of a former slave. He became Dean of Marsh Chapel at Boston University and was a mentor for Martin Luther King Jr. Thurman is reported by Gil Bailie to have said, "Don't ask yourself what the world needs. Ask yourself what makes you come alive, and go do that because what the world needs is people who have come alive."[56]

## In Work, Pursue Your Passion

In essence, Thurman said that the most important thing you can do is follow your dream and passion. It is God Himself who forms these "desires of our heart," and in the Psalms, we are told, "Delight yourself also in the LORD, and He shall give you the desires of your

---

56  https://quoteinvestigator.com/2021/07/09/come-alive/

heart. Commit your way to the LORD, trust also in Him, and He shall bring it to pass" (Psalm 37:4–5).

Often people provide career advice along the lines of we need more rural doctors, economists, and teachers, or there are great opportunities for making money in banking or law. Ideally, everyone needs to find a job where they love what they do because then they will never have to work again. Each day of work will seem like play. Of course, this is an ideal, and there is a reason why it is called work, not play.

When I was leaving school, many of my age group were advised to go into geology because, with increased mining exploration in the country, there were many well-paid job opportunities. At the time, I ignored the advice and pursued my passion for healing animals. This was fortunate because by the time I had graduated, geologists were in over-supply, and a friend who had battled through a geology degree ended up working in a furniture store.

Many people are afraid to pursue their passion for many reasons, including thinking it is unrealistic or impractical. However, in following an area of interest and passion, doors can open to new opportunities and jobs that may not have ever been considered. I talked recently to a man who had developed a successful solar system installation business. He had left school at 14 to become apprenticed as a butcher. He completed that training but then, due to some of the qualifications he acquired during training, found an opportunity to do further training as an electrician. This led to him establishing his own electrical business, including the installation of power poles and then, over time, solar systems. He has become a recognized expert and has developed a large and prosperous business with many employees.

We were all created to do something unique with the talents and skills given to us by God. It is essential to explore and discover what we love and what we are passionate about. As Howard Thurman said, finding what makes us come alive.

## God Gives Adam Work

The story of Creation itself grounds us in the significance of work. The account tells us that after God formed man, He "planted a garden eastward in Eden, and there He put the man whom He had formed" (Genesis 2:8). Then we are told, "The Lord God took the man and put him in the garden of Eden to work it and keep it" (Genesis 2:15). The Hebrew word translated as work is עָבַד transliterated as ʿâbad, and this has the same root as the word for servant. In various Bible translations, rather than work, the translators have used terms such as tend, dress, cultivate, and till. God created man for the work of tending to the Garden, which was beneficial for both the Garden and Adam. God's only rule was not to eat the fruit of the tree of the knowledge of good and evil. This instruction was broken by Eve and Adam through the deception of the serpent. Adam and Eve's choice somehow altered the harmonious fabric of creation. The consequence was a bitter struggle in a hostile environment rather than living and working in harmony with creation. God tells Adam his punishment will be a continuous battle against the natural environment:

"Cursed is the ground for your sake;

In toil you shall eat of it

All the days of your life.

Both thorns and thistles it shall bring forth for you,

And you shall eat the herb of the field.

In the sweat of your face you shall eat bread

Till you return to the ground ..." (Genesis 3:17–19).

Stewarding and tending to creation is God's original desire for humanity. However, the curse upon the ground, due to Adam and Eve's disobedience, turned the work from a harmonious joy to hard labor for survival. Farmers experience this curse firsthand, but the general effect of the curse is the struggle we all experience today in work. Having spent many years farming, fighting against weeds, and trying to raise sheep and cattle during drought and flood, I experienced firsthand the nature of this ongoing battle. Nonetheless, we are created to contribute in a meaningful way to the world around us. St. Paul even wrote an essential instruction to the early church: "If anyone will not work, neither shall he eat" (2 Thessalonians 3:10).

In the case of work, this intersects with the law of sowing and reaping—"whatever a man sows, that he will also reap" (Galatians 6:7). The law of sowing and reaping cannot be avoided in the natural order and is relevant to all facets of life.

I saw this law implemented in a way that seemed extreme to me at the time, but I have since recognized the wisdom of the decision. A friend's son had finished school and refused to apply for jobs or even unemployment benefits. After trying hard over many months to motivate his son to do something, he decided he had to take radical action. He dropped his son off on the main highway in the national capital with a bag of possessions and a few hundred dollars and told him to make his way in life. The son had been warned for some period about this consequence if he failed to try to find a job. Few parents would have the courage to take this action. Although my friend didn't hear from the son for a few years, he eventually regained contact and discovered that the young man had made his way to another part of the country where he had rented a house and found financial support. My friend reasoned that if he had left him at home, it would have been destructive for the young man and for the whole family. It is an extraordinary example of an uncompromising approach to the precept that if you don't work, you don't eat. Interestingly, my friend is not a Christian and not familiar with the Bible, but this truth still informed how he viewed the world. If we don't recognize the natural laws that God Himself has set in place and instead try to soften the consequences of these laws, we will face a battle that we can never win and will be destructive to all involved.

God's plan, though, was to provide Adam with meaningful work, and the Bible offers the following advice:
"Delight yourself also in the LORD,
And He shall give you the desires of your heart.
Commit your way to the LORD,
Trust also in Him,
And He shall bring it to pass" (Psalm 37:4–5).

God has created each of us individually and for a unique role in the world. Remarkably enough, the Bible says that if we learn to know God and focus on Him and His ways, He will give us the desires of our hearts. If we commit our ways to Him, He will bring our desires to pass. God has created each of us with unique capabilities and desires. If we seek to know Him and ask for His guidance, we can be sure that He will respond—often in the most surprising way. Our part is to ask God for His guidance and wisdom and then to be alert to His leading, watching to see what comes our way and which doors may open to us.

# Learning to Work

In earlier times, many families were involved in farming. The long school holidays in the North American summer were implemented, at least partly, so that children could be home to help bring in the farm harvests. In my case, from the age of five, I had to work hard, and my daily chores included milking the cow, using the separator to take the cream, and caring for the chickens and turkeys. I also helped with the sheep work, taking my pony out to muster and working in the sheep yards. It was hard work, but it gave me an understanding from an early age of the idea that "if you don't work, you don't eat." Most other children from local farming families had similar experiences. This was also the norm in most U.S. families at a time when many families were involved in some form of agriculture. Many families also had a vegetable garden or kept poultry in their backyards at the time, so children learned the idea of working to eat. As cities expanded, this became less possible, and children became creatures of apartment blocks, with television as a childminder. In the 1980s, computer games arrived, and children became fully occupied playing video and computer games, and today spend their time posting Instagram photos or making TikTok videos.

It is vital for parents to understand the critical role learning to work plays in developing adults who are independent and able to take responsibility. Though written about a period in the early 1900s in the West of the U.S., the remarkable series of books by Ralph Moody, *Little Britches*,[57] provide many extraordinary and arresting lessons about the value of hard work and family. I highly recommend all eight books in this series, which are important

---

57  https://little-britches-series.fandom.com/wiki/Ralph_Moody

and compelling real-life stories for all the family to read together. The books demonstrate the role of parents in nurturing character in their children and how hardship develops resilience. The books also show the importance of meaningful work, following the passion in your heart, and the way that even children can contribute in a meaningful way to the provision of sustenance for the family.

Starting with simple things is a good idea to prepare children for life and work. In his book about doing things that can change your life, Admiral William H. McRaven[58] notes the importance of simply making your bed in the morning. Learning to take responsibility for our lives is also a theme running through Jordan Peterson's excellent book *12 Rules for Life*.[59]

It is crucial for parents to model and teach children and prepare them for work by finding meaningful tasks for them to contribute to family life and take responsibility early on. These life lessons of working in a safe and close community have long-lasting value for deepening family relationships, developing self-esteem and character, learning independence and responsibility, submitting to authority, and learning to work in a team.

## Working Hard

In the Book of Ecclesiastes (9:10), King Solomon provides an essential perspective about working hard: "Whatever your hand finds to do, do it with your might; for there is no work or device or knowledge or wisdom in the grave where you are going."

---

58  https://www.amazon.com/Make-Your-Bed-Little-Things-ebook/dp/B01KFJGT50

59  https://www.amazon.com/12-Rules-Life-Antidote-Chaos/dp/0345816021

There is quite profound wisdom in this verse, even though it appears initially self-evident. He notes that once we are dead, further work is impossible, so we need to be wholehearted and diligent and work hard while we are alive. Working hard involves applying ourselves to our tasks and working to achieve an excellent outcome. It is difficult to work hard in areas where we have no interest or ability, but a core principle is to learn to constantly work to the best of our ability. There are rewards for diligence, even if they are not immediately evident.

Similarly, it is essential always to be conscientious in the workplace and to avoid gossip and idle chatter. King Solomon writes about this:

"In all labor there is profit,
But idle chatter leads only to poverty" (Proverbs 14:23).

With work, it is essential to show yourself to be a person who delivers more than may be expected. It is important to arrive at work early and to work hard during the day. Looking for ways to help others where you can is essential because most people are only interested in themselves. In the workplace, the most important quality to be known for is your responsibility and reliability in doing what you say you will do. Many people are prepared to work hard for a time but then move from project to project without completing a task. Working hard and being reliable will help you stand out in the workplace. These qualities also strengthen your own will and self-respect, and sense of achievement.

Interestingly, Solomon writes about "idle chatter leading to poverty." Not only does idle chatter or gossip waste time and result in less work being accomplished, but it can have many other negative impacts in the workplace. The dangers of gossip are highlighted throughout the Book of Proverbs:

"A perverse man sows strife,
And a whisperer separates the best of friends" (Proverbs 16:28).

"He who goes about as a talebearer reveals secrets;
Therefore do not associate with one who flatters with his lips" (Proverbs 20:19).

"Where there is no wood, the fire goes out;
And where there is no talebearer, strife ceases" (Proverbs 26:20).

Gossip is alluring, which is why various Royal Family "secrets" seem to gain so much attention in the media. Ancient wisdom tells us to keep well away from people prone to gossip. Not only will it affect our work, but it will likely negatively impact us and draw us into the strife and disharmony that occurs in the workplace when gossip abounds.

## The Lure of Laziness

It is easy to develop lazy habits in the modern world. For most people in the West, we don't have to work hard physically to acquire food, and now people can even work from home and never have to get out of their pajamas. There are many distractors: social media, online movies, phone calls, and myriad diversions that can lead us away from completing our work. The old saying is true: "The hardest part of any job is making a start." Laziness is a lure or trap and can be appealing because when it is difficult to make a start on a work project, an attractive alternative is to become side-tracked. Laziness is also a habit that can be developed during teenage years when, without clear boundaries or responsibility for tasks set by parents, young people can vegetate in their rooms and drift into a virtual world. The best way to beat the virtual world is a good dose of reality—a job and hard work. Advice about the danger of laziness is reiterated throughout the Book of Proverbs and seems to be one of the most important areas of advice from the king to his son. Here are some of the most important verses that deal with laziness:

- "As vinegar to the teeth and smoke to the eyes,
  So is the lazy man to those who send him." (Proverbs 10:26)

- "The hand of the diligent will rule,
  But the lazy man will be put to forced labor." (Proverbs 12:24)

- "The lazy man does not roast what he took in hunting,
  But diligence is man's precious possession." (Proverbs 12:27)

- "The soul of a lazy man desires, and has nothing;
  But the soul of the diligent shall be made rich." (Proverbs 13:4)

- "The way of the lazy man is like a hedge of thorns,
  But the way of the upright is a highway." (Proverbs 15:19)

- "Laziness casts one into a deep sleep,
  And an idle person will suffer hunger." (Proverbs 19:15)

- "A lazy man buries his hand in the bowl,
  And will not so much as bring it to his mouth again." (Proverbs 19:24)

- "The lazy man will not plow because of winter;
  He will beg during harvest and have nothing." (Proverbs 20:4)

- "The desire of the lazy man kills him,
  For his hands refuse to labor." (Proverbs 21:25)

- "I went by the field of the lazy man,

  And by the vineyard of the man devoid of understanding;

  And there it was, all overgrown with thorns;

  Its surface was covered with nettles;

  Its stone wall was broken down.

  When I saw it, I considered it well;

  I looked on it and received instruction:

  A little sleep, a little slumber,

  A little folding of the hands to rest;

  So shall your poverty come like a prowler,

  And your need like an armed man." (Proverbs 24:30–34)

- "As a door turns on its hinges,

  So does the lazy man on his bed." (Proverbs 26:14)

It is worthwhile reading through these verses several times as they each offer a different perspective on the danger and lure of laziness. Laziness is a vice that brings tears to those in authority who send a lazy person to do a task. A reluctance to get off your bed and complete work will have many downstream effects, damaging personal well-being. Ultimately, a lazy person's impact is seen in how they live: their property, appearance, and possessions fall into disrepair, and this leads to poverty and perhaps even death.

# Wisdom in Dealing With Authority

Most of us have experienced bad bosses at work. Being under authority can often be very difficult, and there are many pitfalls in dealing with management at work. The Bible provides us with a challenging but profound insight into authority. Romans 13:1 tells us:

"Let every soul be subject to the governing authorities. For there is no authority except from God, and the authorities that exist are appointed by God. Therefore whoever resists the authority resists the ordinance of God, and those who resist will bring judgment on themselves."

In this verse, St Paul is saying that God has set up all authority and that, ultimately, all authority is accountable to Him. Therefore, when we resist authority, we can find ourselves inadvertently resisting God. All of us find it difficult to be under authority, but being respectful and obedient to the people who are placed in authority over us will bring its blessings. [The proviso, of course, is that the commands of those in authority are not in conflict with those of God, in which case various accounts in the Bible, including in the Book of Acts, teach us that we need to "obey God rather than men" (Acts 5:29). However, it should be remembered that these cases tend to be rare.] Our first instinct must be to submit to the authority over us and be obedient to what we are asked to do. There is an old saying that "our attitude determines our altitude," and so we must have a good attitude in responding to directions. Otherwise, our career path will be down rather than up. After working for many organizations with different types of bosses, these are a few tips that I have picked up about dealing well with authority in the workplace:

- **It is essential to understand your roles and responsibilities**. Many organizations have position descriptions that are many pages long. However, usually, just a few areas are important for your boss. It is good to ask your boss, "What are the most important things for me to achieve so that you will consider my work a success?" Most bosses will have a clear idea of what is most important to them in the role that you are taking on.

- **Understand and adhere to the company's policies and procedures**. These policies are primarily common sense but have become increasingly multifaceted and lengthy as companies have sought to address many complex social issues.

- **Be reliable and meet deadlines**. It is important to meet deadlines. For bosses, the best predictor of future behavior is past behavior, so if you find yourself missing deadlines and making excuses, your boss can assume that you will do this again. However, if the deadline is unreasonable, it is best to indicate this up front and not wait until the project is overdue.

- **Be receptive to feedback**. One of my favorite sayings is that "feedback is the breakfast of champions, but only if you are tough enough to eat it!" It is important to be receptive to feedback from your boss. They may have different ideas from you about how a job is to be done but remember that they are the boss.

- **Find a mentor**. It doesn't take long when you join any organization to see those older and more experienced than you who are well-regarded. Ask one of these successful people to be a mentor. One of the simplest things to do is to take them out for coffee once a month and ask them questions about the organization, what they have learned, and how to be successful.

- **Learn teamwork**. Most workplaces require teamwork, and it is crucial to learn how to work effectively with the others in your team. Demonstrate to your boss your broader value to the team by building relationships rather than just doing the work. Doing this may require some social time outside work so that you can better know and understand team members and their challenges. It also allows you to identify people's strengths so that you can work with your colleagues more effectively.

## The Importance of Rest

Notably, God built the idea of a sabbath rest into the fabric of creation. After six days of creation, God rested on the seventh day, and the Bible tells us that: "Then God blessed the seventh day and sanctified it, because in it He rested from all His work which God had created and made" (Genesis 2:3). In Jewish tradition, the seventh day (Shabbat) starts at sundown on Friday and ends at sunset on Saturday. The Sabbath is important and holy (set aside) to the Lord. From the beginning, a sabbath has been a non-negotiable part of God's creation and also is listed as one of the Ten Commandments: "Remember the Sabbath day, to keep it holy. Six days you shall labor and do all your work, but the seventh day is the Sabbath of the LORD your God. In it you shall do no work: you, nor your son, nor your daughter, nor your male servant, nor your female servant, nor your cattle, nor your stranger who is within your gates" (Exodus 20:8–10).

It is fascinating to be in Israel on Shabbat and to see how seriously this rest is taken. In the West, Sunday has traditionally been the day of rest, but increasingly, rest is ignored in a society where life is lived at a frenetic pace.

There is much focus in workplaces today on work-life balance. This is a somewhat wrong focus as there are seasons of work where long hours are necessary and other seasons where there is less pressure. However, God is serious about His Sabbath and instructs that the rest should involve everyone in your household, even your animals. The day is to be kept holy (Hebrew word קָדַשׁ qâḏaš—meaning dedicated, set apart, purified, separate, or honored). If we want to align ourselves with God's blessings, then a day of rest dedicated to Him is critical for success. At the most superficial level, we are created for both work and rest. Too little or too much of either will have a negative impact on our health and well-being.

## KEY POINTS ABOUT WISDOM IN WORK

- In decisions about your career and work, the best advice is to pursue your passion and work in an area that makes you feel strong (brings you a sense of life).

- Work is essential for our well-being and was fashioned into our makeup by God. Our ancestors' rebellion in the Garden resulted in us having to battle with "thorns and thistles," but working, as far as we can, in areas of our passion and skills is beneficial for our well-being.

- "Delight yourself in the Lord and He will give you the desires of your heart" (Psalm 37:4). As we grow in knowing and delighting in God, His desires and ways will begin to flourish in our hearts as our own desires.

- We need to learn to work, and parents need to help children understand the role of work and to encourage them to take responsibility in the family.

- Working hard and being conscientious is vital in all work tasks. Gossip in the workplace is dangerous to the quality of your work and relationships.

165

- For each of us, learning to be under authority is vital to our character development. Ultimately, we are all under God's authority.

- Sabbath rest is part of God's design in creation. We need to learn how to set aside a sabbath free of work or distracting electronic communications and keep this day for the Lord and for personal restoration.

- God designed work for our benefit, and we need to work to achieve excellence in areas that, where possible, bring joy and delight to our hearts. However, wherever we work, even in jobs that we don't like, if we have a good attitude, we will benefit, and our character and attitude will be recognized. It is worthwhile us taking leaves out of the biblical stories of Joseph and Daniel, who thrived in oppressive conditions in Egypt and Babylon, respectively, because of their excellent attitude, personal diligence, and hard work.

Work allows us to earn money so that we have food and shelter and can provide for our families. Money, one of the essential outcomes of work, is our focus in the next chapter of the journey of wisdom we are taking together.

# CHAPTER 11
## WISDOM AND MONEY

*"A good name is to be chosen rather than great riches, loving favor rather than silver or gold." (Proverbs 22:1)*

A much-quoted story in my family concerns my grandfather and the battle he faced on the farm during the Depression years of the 1930s. Finances were tight, and farm produce was worth very little. My grandfather was talking to a friend who was a local farmer and who was complaining about the challenge of having too much money. He said:

"Money's a worry, Reub."

My grandfather's response was:

"It's a bloody worry when you haven't got any!"

The lack of money is a daily test for most of us; issues like inflation, recession, the housing crisis, and insufficient funds to feed our families and pay bills cause stress and anxiety. The ancient writers of the Bible recognized the difficulties of managing money and its hold on us. King Solomon, who was the wealthiest and greatest king of all time, summed up the situation of wealth when he wrote: "For there is a man whose labor is with wisdom, knowledge, and skill; yet he must leave his heritage to a man who has not labored for it ..." (Ecclesiastes 2:21).

The adage that one generation makes the wealth and the next generation spends it seems one of the truths of life. Solomon noted that even if we work hard and gain much, the road isn't easy, and, in the end, what do we gain?

"Wisdom and money can get you almost anything, but only wisdom can save your life." (Ecclesiastes 7:12 NLT)

What is a wise approach to money, and what are the secrets to contentment in relation to our finances? In this chapter, we will explore some ideas from the Bible that provide a framework for understanding and dealing wisely with money.

## The Love of Money

We are inclined to think that money and possessions are simply objects with no meaning beyond what they can give us. Yet the Bible writers provide many warnings about the dangers we face when money is elevated to primacy in our lives. In St. Paul's letter to young Timothy, he gives significant wisdom on the issue of money. He writes about the importance of being content because "we brought nothing into the world, and it is certain that we carry nothing out" (1 Timothy 6:7). He explains that a desire to be rich can become a temptation (a spiritual trap), a desire that can lead to evil and thence to destruction. Then Paul writes:

"For the love of money is a root of all kinds of evil, for which some have strayed from the faith in their greediness, and pierced themselves through with many sorrows" (1 Timothy 6:10).

This is an important verse that is often misquoted. Money is not the root of all evil but rather the **love** of money. If the lure of money leads to greed, then we are inviting trouble for ourselves with "many sorrows." Money and the things that can be acquired are a snare and trap if money dominates our lives. There is something about the power of money because it can control us and make us a slave to the money rather than its master. About 1,000 years before St. Paul, King Solomon brought God's wisdom on this in the Book of Ecclesiastes: "Those who love money will never have enough. How meaningless to think that wealth brings true happiness!" (Ecclesiastes 5:10 NLT).

Somehow, we need to have a healthy respect for money, which is necessary for daily living, but avoid money becoming the love of our lives because when it dominates us, it will lead to slavery, and happiness will be impossible.

Now if you were ever to talk to anyone and ask, "Do you love money?" the answer would invariably be "No." Yet whether we are aware of it or not, the love of money seeks to control us, which is a spiritual dynamic. The New Testament contains Jesus' teaching on this, and a substantial section of Jesus' Sermon on the Mount (Matthew 5–7) brings wisdom and perspective on money and wealth. Jesus says to the large crowd gathered on a hillside near Capernaum:

"Do not lay up for yourselves treasures on earth, where moth and rust destroy and where thieves break in and steal; but lay up for yourselves treasures in heaven, where neither moth nor rust destroys and where thieves do not break in and steal. For where your treasure is, there your heart will be also" (Matthew 6:19–21).

His warning to the crowd is as true today as it was in Galilee 2,000 years ago. If we focus on the "treasures" of life—money, clothes, cars, the latest phones, houses, boats, jewelry, holiday homes, crypto currency, land, and even fame—all these things can be destroyed. Daily we hear about thieves breaking into homes and

169

stealing possessions, hackers raiding bank accounts, billions lost in cryptocurrencies, drought ravaging the land of farmers, mouse plagues and locusts destroying crops, stock market crashes, and houses being lost because of an increase in interest rates. These are the modern equivalents of destruction by "moth and rust." Jesus diagnoses the core issue in this famous line: "For where your treasure is, there your heart will be also" (Matthew 6:21). In essence, what we value most highly, think about, desire, give attention to, and spend our time on and even covet is our "treasure." All of us have areas like this in our lives, and while it may not be money, there will be proxies for money that we may inadvertently allow to dominate our lives. The power of various "treasures" to dominate and control us is well demonstrated in the *Lord of the Rings* films where Gollum speaks about his "precious"—the ring. That which we allow to direct and control us will ultimately enslave us.

Jesus' remedy was simple but challenging: "Lay up for yourselves treasures in heaven" (Matthew 6:20). He said these treasures were eternal and indestructible. One thing is sure— we need to know what these "treasures in heaven" are and how to obtain them. One thing we can see as we read through the Bible is that the "treasures" that Jesus spoke about are not physical but hidden in a person's heart (Matthew 6:21, 12:35; Luke 6:45). It seems that the accounting for these hidden "treasures" is kept in heaven. The simple foundation for the storing up of these treasures arises from the wisdom Jesus provided when asked about the greatest of God's commandments. He said: "You shall love the LORD your God with all your heart, with all your soul, and with all your mind. This is the first and great commandment. And the second is like it: You shall love your neighbor as yourself" (Matthew 22:37–39).

We can store up treasure in heaven by loving God first and then loving our neighbors. These deceptively simple words defy us daily because our human nature is biased towards self-interest. Fortunately, what is impossible with us is possible with God. If we give our lives to God and are born again by His Spirit (John 3:3), we are brought into His family and kingdom and set on the path of learning to live by the power of another life (Galatians 2:20). This is both a simple and complex matter. It is talked about in many places in the New Testament and an excellent book, *The Normal Christian Life*, published in the 1950s by a Chinese Christian, Watchman Nee.[60]

We all need to understand the spiritual power of the love of money and possessions and the tendency of these things to enslave us. The remedy is to ensure that God Himself is put into first place in our lives. We will find that learning how to do this is often a journey, but if this is our desire, He will help us.

# Giving

Giving first to God was a foundational principle of ancient Hebrew society and is described in many places in the Old Testament. One of the places it was highlighted was when the different territories were assigned to the 12 tribes of Israel after they had entered the Promised Land. The priestly tribe, Levi, was given no specific region but instead was to rely on God for their support, which came through offerings provided by the other tribes. You could say that this was the first example of a "handout culture," but the priests had critical work in the nation to "minister to the Lord" (Leviticus 7:35). The other 11 tribes supported this work fully, and upon this rested the success and prosperity of the nation.

---

60 https://tochrist.org/Doc/Books/Watchman%20Nee/The%20Normal%20Christian%20Life.pdf

King Solomon had immense wealth and wrote:

"Honor the LORD with your wealth

and with the best part of everything you produce.

Then he will fill your barns with grain,

and your vats will overflow with good wine" (Proverbs 3:9–10).

The principle is simple—because He has created us and enables us to accumulate wealth, it is right to love Him and honor Him as the source of all our provision by giving back to Him the best of what we have earned. In the Book of Deuteronomy, God gives some specific instructions about giving one-tenth or a "tithe" to Him and to the support of His priests and also to widows, orphans, and foreigners living in the land (Deuteronomy 14:22–29).

In the last book of the Old Testament, the Book of Malachi, God surprisingly asks His people to test Him in this matter of giving back to Him. In Malachi 3:10, God says:

"'Bring all the tithes into the storehouse,

That there may be food in My house,

And try Me now in this,'

Says the LORD of hosts,

'If I will not open for you the windows of heaven

And pour out for you such blessing

That there will not be room enough to receive it'" (Malachi 3:10).

Even when we are struggling financially, the solution is to give our tithe to God, to support what He is doing on the earth, and this can be done in a range of ways. This culture of giving and giving generously is most well-established in the U.S., where U.S. citizens give billions annually to a range of Christian works, missions, and charitable causes. Undoubtedly, much of the prosperity in the U.S. since its founding almost 250 years ago has been related to the culture of generous giving to those in need and tithing. Such generosity is not found in many other Western countries, where there is a belief that caring for others and charitable works is the government's responsibility.

The Old Testament not only speaks about tithing but related to this are two concepts largely unknown in the modern world: the Shmita (sabbatical) year for the land (Leviticus 25:1–7) and Yovel (the Year of Jubilee) outlined in Leviticus 25:8–55. The Shmita or sabbatical year is every seventh year, and the land was not to be worked for agriculture but instead left fallow so that any plants that grew could be used by the poor or eaten by wild animals. The Yovel or Jubilee year took place at the end of seven cycles of seven years (the 50th year) and required that not only was the land rested but that any land sold was returned to its previous owners, slaves were set free, and debts were forgiven. As with tithing, the principle that God is teaching us through Sabbath years is that everything belongs to Him and that our wealth and sustenance come from Him. It is vital to relinquish back into His hands a portion of that which He has given to us. Also, there is rest and restoration for the land itself. In the Old Testament, we find that the Shmita and Yovel were not consistently observed during the years in the Promised Land, and, as a result, the children of Israel were eventually sent into exile, at least in part, to reclaim and restore a time of rest for the land (2 Chronicles 36:21).

These foundational precepts of God have been mostly lost from modern culture and can only be to our detriment. However, some vestiges remain, and while teaching at the university, I benefited from several sabbatical periods, where I was able to travel to overseas universities, learn new ideas, and be refreshed. As a result, I became a more effective teacher and researcher. The

Shmita and Yovel are counterintuitive to our human ways of operating, but God's ways from ancient times are undoubtedly the ways of wisdom. As paradoxical as it may seem, gaining wealth by giving or resting is a foundation of wisdom for success in life.

# Stewardship

The concept of stewardship has been evident from the earliest days of creation. Genesis 2:15 tells us: "And the Lord God took the man and put him in the Garden of Eden to tend and guard and keep it" (Genesis 2:15 AMP). The Hebrew word שָׁמַר transliterated as šâmar, means: to guard, keep, reserve, preserve, and watch over. A good English equivalent for all these words is "steward," which has the sense of looking after something for another. Being a steward of God's creation is part of God's intention, and this also applies to our possessions and money.

King Solomon wrote about the importance of diligence and saving in the approach to money. I like this translation from the New Living Translation, which provides modern wording:
"Wealth from get-rich-quick schemes quickly disappears;
wealth from hard work grows over time" (Proverbs 13:11 NLT).

The road to creating wealth is established by saving our earnings over time and putting aside at least a tithe for God and a tithe for saving and growth. In our debt-based financial system, the ready availability of credit has created a modern culture of spending first and thinking and paying later. The result is an extraordinary level of debt as well as the creation of a culture of greed and hedonism. This is well expressed in the old song of the rock-group Queen, that says: "I want it all, and I want it now!"

It is interesting that Jesus taught in parables, and many parables had an agricultural theme. Jesus' parables are interesting because all are real-life stories, but often the stories can be hard to understand, especially for modern readers who are removed from the land and that culture. Jesus, Himself says that his parables are designed to conceal things from those unwilling to understand, and after telling the parable of the sower (Matthew 13:1-9), which is discussed below, Jesus says: "I speak to them in parables, because seeing they do not see, and hearing they do not hear, nor do they understand" (Matthew 13:13).

The parable of the talents (Matthew 25:14–30), which is about stewardship of wealth, has received much attention and analysis from Bible scholars. The parable of the talents was told by Jesus shortly before His arrest and crucifixion, and it followed immediately after His teaching to his disciples about His return or second coming to the earth.

"For the kingdom of heaven is like a man traveling to a far country, who called his own servants and delivered his goods to them. And to one he gave five talents, to another two, and to another one, to each according to his own ability; and immediately he went on a journey. Then he who had received the five talents went and traded with them, and made another five talents. And likewise he who had received two gained two more also. But he who had received one went and dug in the ground, and hid his lord's money. After a long time the lord of those servants came and settled accounts with them.

"So he who had received five talents came and brought five other talents, saying, 'Lord, you delivered to me five talents; look, I have gained five more talents besides them.' His lord said to him, 'Well done, good and faithful servant; you were faithful over a few things; I will make you ruler over many things. Enter into the joy of your lord.' He also who had received two talents came and said, 'Lord, you delivered to me two talents; look, I have gained two more talents besides them.' His lord said to him, 'Well done, good and faithful servant; you have been faithful over a few things; I will make you ruler over many things. Enter into the joy of your lord.'

"Then he who had received the one talent came and said, 'Lord, I knew you to be a hard man, reaping where you have not sown, and gathering where you have not scattered seed. And I was afraid, and went and hid your talent in the ground. Look, there you have what is yours.'

"But his lord answered and said to him, 'You wicked and lazy servant, you knew that I reap where I have not sown, and gather where I have not scattered seed. So you ought to have deposited my money with the bankers, and at my coming I would have received back my own with interest. So take the talent from him, and give it to him who has ten talents.'

"For to everyone who has, more will be given, and he will have abundance; but from him who does not have, even what he has will be taken away. And cast the unprofitable servant into the outer darkness. There will be weeping and gnashing of teeth" (Matthew 25:14–30).

Jesus says something quite extraordinary in response to the disciples' question about the use of parables. He tells them that those who are His disciples and genuinely seek to be taught by Him have been given the gift of understanding the kingdom of God. Understandably, the parables caused a degree of confusion among Jesus' listeners, who were trying to understand the significance of the stories that Jesus told them.

So, about the disciples' questions about the somewhat cryptic nature of the parables, Jesus says to them: "He answered and said to them, 'Because it has been given to you to know the mysteries of the kingdom of heaven, but to them it has not been given. For whoever has, to him more will be given, and he will have abundance; but whoever does not have, even what he has will be taken away from him'" (Matthew 13:11–12).

The essence of what Jesus is saying is that it requires diligence and effort to seek after and discover things of the kingdom of God, and to those who do, more will be given. In contrast, those who do not seek the kingdom of God will become spiritually poor. This is counterintuitive to us raised on a Robin Hood philosophy of taking from the rich and giving to the poor. Essentially, God is telling those who become spiritually rich through their wholehearted pursuit of God will ultimately receive even more abundance, but those who have not sought Him and so have essentially nothing, even that will be taken away.

So, returning to the parable of the talents, Jesus is teaching His disciples about wise stewardship. The English word "talent," used in modern times to describe a natural ability, appears to have been first used in this way in the 9th century, but this modern use of the word is still relevant to the parable. However, at the time that Jesus told this parable, a talent was a weight, usually of gold or silver, with enormous value. Some estimates put this at around 20 years of an average wage. In the parable, three servants were given three different amounts of money when their master went away. Though there were three different amounts of money, even the smallest amount represented an enormous sum. Two of the three who were given the most considerable amounts of wealth invested and multiplied the amounts given. The third person, who received the least amount (but still probably around $1 million in today's currency), does nothing except hide the money and keep it secure.

The return of the master brings with it harsh judgment for this third servant, who did not steward wisely what he had been given.

There are several essential elements to the parable of the talents, but concerning the focus of this chapter on money, here are a few points from Jesus' teaching about wisdom with money:

1. Everything comes from God, so we must wisely use the "talents" (wealth and abilities) that we have been given and not squander them or waste them by not putting them to good use.

2. Diligence and hard work are necessary to increase the value of what we have been given by God.

3. Complacency and fear are barriers to multiplying what we have been given for God's purposes on the earth, as demonstrated by the third servant, who, in his state of fear, did nothing with the talent and incurred his master's wrath.

4. We are all accountable for what we have been given, and in the parable of the talents, Jesus points forward to a day of reckoning. If we do nothing with what we have been given, there will ultimately be harsh judgment, and what we have will be given to those who were diligent and hard-working.

There can occur times in life when we all need a handout. However, what we need more is a hand-up! The old saying, "Give a man a fish, and you feed him for a day; teach a man to fish, and you feed him for a lifetime," is relevant in this stewardship story. Each of us has God-given abilities, and the way of wisdom is to work hard, steward well what we have been given, and create wealth, material and spiritual, that can be used for God's kingdom purposes.

Knowing how to manage money is essential, and to help in this area, I have given many young people a copy of George S. Clason's

1926 classic *The Richest Man in Babylon.*[61] The book is written as a parable but demonstrates in an easy-to-understand format the importance of spending less than you earn, saving ten percent of what you earn, and investing wisely. This may sound simple, but it isn't familiar to our system of easy credit. The main lessons from the book include: paying yourself first, living within your means, putting your money to work, keeping your money safe, becoming a homeowner, ensuring your future income, and improving your skills to earn more income. The book is short and is a money-managing classic that can benefit anyone at any stage of life.

## Contentment

An essential piece of wisdom from ancient times about wealth and money is the principle of contentment. Proverbs 15:16 puts this idea simply: "Better is a little with the fear of the LORD, Than great treasure with trouble."

The writer of Hebrews amplifies this principle when he writes: "Don't love money; be satisfied with what you have. For God has said, 'I will never fail you. I will never abandon you'" (Hebrews 13:5 NLT).

For those who choose to put their trust in God, this latter promise is wonderful and seems to derive in part from Moses' final words to Joshua and the children of Israel as they were about to enter the Promised Land (Deuteronomy 31:6, 8).

The great St. Paul provides an excellent model of the secret of contentment, even in challenging circumstances. While in prison and facing death, he wrote to the Philippians, "For I have learned how to be content with whatever I have. I know how to live on almost nothing or with everything. I have learned

---

61  https://wealthynickel.com/lessons-from-the-richest-man-in-babylon/

the secret of living in every situation, whether it is with a full stomach or empty, with plenty or little. For I can do everything through Christ, who gives me strength" (Philippians 4:11–13 NLT).

This is our challenge with money and our possessions, or lack of them. The way of God's ancient wisdom is to be diligent, work hard, give generously, not let money dominate us, and be content in all circumstances. This is because we trust in God, who strengthens us in every situation.

# KEY POINTS ABOUT WISDOM AND MONEY

- Ultimately, it is wise to recognize that if we focus on money and possessions, one day, we will die, and as the old saying puts it, "You can't take it with you." I saw a memorable interpretation of this recently when I read: "You don't see a U-Haul trailer behind a hearse."

- It is essential to understand that the love of money and wealth has a spiritual dimension and can exert an invisible grip on us and enslave us. King Solomon wrote that: "Those who love money will never have enough. How meaningless to think that wealth brings true happiness!" (Ecclesiastes 5:10 NLT).

- Jesus told His followers that "where your treasure is, there is your heart also" (Matthew 6:21). We all need to understand what it is that we treasure because often, we will find that it is at odds with real and eternal treasure.

- God teaches us a paradox in the Bible that the secret to wealth lies in giving generously to God and others.

- It is essential to recognize that we are all stewards of God-given resources. Each of us has God-given abilities, and the way of wisdom is to work hard, steward well what we have been given, and create wealth that can be used for God's kingdom purposes.

Having considered wisdom in education, work, and money, we will look at some bigger-picture areas related to wisdom. In the next chapter, we will focus on wisdom in leadership.

# CHAPTER 12
# WISDOM IN LEADERSHIP

*"And He sat down, called the twelve, and said to them, 'If anyone desires to be first, he shall be last of all and servant of all.'" (Mark 9:35)*

Understanding leadership is at the very heart of wisdom. We all have leadership roles and influence, even if it is learning how to lead ourselves. Learning how to lead and understanding the keys to leadership are essential components of the journey into wisdom. I believe that understanding leadership is a foundational area for wisdom in the day-to-day areas of life. About twenty years ago, I attended a seminar by U.S. leadership guru Pat Murray,[62] who taught a few simple but profound concepts. At the heart of leadership are two questions: Who am I? What price am I willing to pay to be that person? Many issues lie behind these two questions, but at the start of the road to wisdom is self-knowledge and a commitment to live your life from a place of bedrock principles. There is a price to be paid to become your authentic self rather than someone who wants to please others. You need to be prepared to say no when you need to and not deviate from your "non-negotiables"—those areas where you will not compromise.

---

62  http://www.billdotson.com/2012/06/interview-questions-from-pat-murray/

# Maxwell and Leadership

I have been interested in leadership for the last 25 years and have made a detailed study that has included most of the significant leadership books. My journey started in the late 1990s at a church weekend seminar. During one of the breaks, I visited the bookshop to look for a good spiritual book. My eyes alighted upon a book by John C. Maxwell, remarkably titled *The 21 Irrefutable Laws of Leadership*.[63] I thought what a ridiculous claim and proceeded to thumb through the book to refute the preposterous title. To my shock, I found that the book was outstanding, and the laws were irrefutable! The central thesis of the book was, *"Everything rises and falls on leadership,"* and that *"leadership is influence: nothing more, nothing less."* The book was outstanding in its simplicity and depth of understanding of leadership. I decided there and then that I must read the book, so I bought it.

Over subsequent years, I have read more than 100 books on leadership, but none have managed to highlight the critical areas of leadership as well and simply as *The 21 Irrefutable Laws of Leadership.* Maxwell's definition of leadership as being influence is an essential concept because although we may not be organization leaders, we all can have influence and impact. One of the most important ways of having influence is by learning to ask good questions, which makes the person to whom you are talking search for solutions to issues that they otherwise are unlikely to do.

One of Maxwell's most important laws is the "law of the lid."[64] This law states that a leader's capability limits that of the group they are

63 https://nela.ced.ncsu.edu/wp-content/uploads/2019/06/Book-Summary-%E2%80%93-The-21-Irrefutable.pdf
64 https://daveschoenbeck.com/john-maxwells-leadership-law-1-the-law-of-the-lid/

leading. This law requires a leader to know their limitations and implement development processes to help lift the "lid." Otherwise, Maxwell believes that the team will be limited to the level provided by the leader. He cites the story of the McDonald brothers, originators of the system that developed into the now worldwide fast-food chain McDonalds. The brothers had an excellent concept but did not have the level of leadership to develop the business into the extraordinary franchise it is today. The person with a higher level of vision and skills was the entrepreneur Ray Kroc.

One can see this most frequently in politics, where the leader's limitations impact the fortunes of their political party. While many politicians may enter politics with lofty intentions, they soon meet the "law of the lid" and the challenges of self-interest. To succeed as a leader, you have to put aside only your self-interest to mobilize people to achieve a bigger purpose.

If, as John C Maxwell says, "Everything rises and falls on leadership," then we must understand what good leadership is, whether it be in politics, business, in our families, or among our friends. This is an important question for us today in politics; in considering leadership, I was drawn to the extraordinary story of Moses, one of the most outstanding biblical leaders. After all, this reluctant leader took about 3 million difficult people on a 40-year camping trip in the desert near Egypt and survived a number of almost impossible circumstances.

## Moses and Leadership

The story of Moses is outlined in the biblical books of Exodus, Leviticus, Numbers, and Deuteronomy. It is worthwhile reading the whole story. Here are a few of the critical details:

- The family of Jacob (also called the children of Israel or the Hebrews) had moved from Canaan to Egypt because of famine. During their time in Egypt, which was 430 years (Exodus 12:40), the family grew from about 70 at the time of Joseph to several million when Moses arrived on the scene. Pharaoh, the ruler of Egypt, realized that these descendants of Jacob could take over the country unless he put them in their place, so the whole nation was enslaved in Egypt.

- The Bible tells us that "their cry came up to God because of the bondage." God is not an impartial God who looks on without interest but hears the cry of His people and those who call upon Him, and He intervenes and acts in history.

- The deliverance of Noah and Moses has significant parallels. Pharaoh had ordered genocide by killing all the male children of Israel. We don't know how many babies died, but the Bible tells us that the midwives did not carry out the command. One particular child, Moses, was put into a basket or ark (תֵּבָה – teva) and providentially ended up being found and raised by Pharaoh's daughter. It is significant that the Hebrew word teva תֵּבָה is only used twice in the Old Testament. The word describes the massive timber ark that saved Noah's family and the small reed basket into which Moses was consigned to the River Nile to await God's providential rescue.

- We don't know any details of Moses' early life, which must have been privileged. Nevertheless, he knew that he was one of the Hebrews because some years later, when he saw an Egyptian striking one of his compatriots, he killed the Egyptian. Pharaoh heard about this and sought to kill Moses, but Moses fled to Midian, which is probably in north-western Saudi Arabia today.

- God's hand was on Moses in Midian because he found himself being taken in by the family of Jethro, a priest of Midian and a wise man who later gave excellent counsel to Moses.

- Moses was a shepherd for 40 years in the desert, and one day was moving sheep when he came to what the Bible calls Horeb (also called Sinai), the mountain of God. On this mountain, God later gave Moses the un-editable Ten Commandments on stone tablets.

- A mysterious figure (called the Angel or Messenger of the Lord) appears to Moses in a burning bush at Sinai, but the bush is not consumed. Moses turns aside to see this wonder, and his life direction changes as God speaks to him from the burning bush.

- God, Himself sees leadership potential in this man who has been wandering around shepherding sheep on the backside of the desert for 40 years. Having been raised as a prince in Egypt, Moses must have been wondering if his life was finished.

- God calls Moses to go to the Pharaoh of Egypt, the most powerful man in the world at that time, and ask him to set His people free. Once free, God instructs Moses to lead them to a "good and broad land, a land flowing with milk and honey" (Exodus 3:8).

- Humanly speaking, it is an impossible job, and the rest of the story in Exodus covers Moses' challenges with Pharaoh, his ultimate success in leading the Hebrews out of Egypt because of a series of outstanding miracles, the subsequent rebellion of the Hebrews against Moses and God, and forty years of wanderings around the desert because of Israel's disobedience.

Exodus's critical and foundational story teaches us much about God, His character, and His sovereignty, particularly when everything looks impossible. There are many lessons for us to learn from the story of Moses, but in the rest of this chapter, I will focus on ten of the most critical leadership lessons that I have taken from the story.

# 10 Leadership Lessons From Moses

1.  **Nothing is impossible with God.** Too often, we can stumble at the first hurdle of life because it seems too difficult. For example, Winston Churchill had a sense of divine destiny to save Britain many years before he became Prime Minister. Still, events and thinking in the 1930s consigned him to the political wilderness, until Hitler invaded Poland. As the old saying has it, "Cometh the hour, cometh the man." A just cause with God's backing will, by faith, overcome the greatest rulers and kingdoms. Of course, you need to know that the call you have heard is from God. History tells us that rather than a call from God, it could be a call from Satan that results in a megalomaniacal sense of delusion and evil. This certainly is the story of evil dictators who often see themselves as gods.

2.  **Past mistakes don't need to disqualify us from leadership.** Many of us make bad decisions in life, but God can use our mistakes and awareness of our brokenness to teach humility and so prepare us for leadership. Moses

killed an Egyptian in an act, apparently, of righteous anger. This resulted in him fleeing for his life. During 40 years of shepherding in the wilderness, he would have learned many lessons from shepherding, understanding the natural order and God's providential intervention. It may be that an elderly man washed up and without hope, is sometimes what God needs to achieve His purposes. We can feel disqualified from leadership because of past failures, but with God, there is always hope because His specialty is redemption.

3. **A wilderness experience is often good ground for leadership preparation.** This was the case with Moses, and although we don't know what happened in the desert, it must have toughened him and taught him obedience to his father-in-law Jethro and humility as he served as a shepherd to what may have been unruly sheep. This would have involved directing their paths, finding feed and water, and tending to injured sheep. These skills would later be vital for Moses in leading a recalcitrant people through the desert.

There are times when we find ourselves in the "wilderness," but often, this is God's gift to us, to mature us, to teach us to depend on Him, and to make us ready for His purposes. In the wilderness of life, everything is stripped away, and there are no comforts or distractions. In the modern world, so many things are vying for our attention that we may need a desert experience to hear God's "still small voice" (1 Kings 19:12), like with the prophet Elijah. We may need a desert experience to hear God's "still small voice" and learn to depend on Him at a deeper level.

4. **Leadership includes obedience.** God's greater purpose is to teach us obedience to Him and His ways. We don't naturally choose God's ways, and God tells the prophet, Isaiah, "For my thoughts are not your thoughts, nor are your ways My ways" (Isaiah 55:8). God's ways don't tend to come naturally to us and often are difficult to understand. God called Jonah to proclaim the destruction of the great city of Nineveh because of the sin of the people of that city, but Jonah headed in the opposite direction. Eventually, God had His way. Jonah brought the message of judgment to Ninevah, and astoundingly, the whole city repented. This was an unexpected result for Jonah (Jonah 3), who wanted to see the city wiped out after he did God's bidding.

Moses did not want the job of delivering and leading the Hebrew people out of Egypt and thought that God should look for someone else. Moses did return to Egypt to fulfil God's plan, and he learned obedience to God in an almost progressive way through ten miraculous and terrible signs, the last of which was the death of all firstborn Egyptians and the firstborn of their livestock (Exodus 11:1-10). Without obedience, there is lawlessness, which God judged harshly when the Israelites rebelled against God and Moses' leadership in the desert. Obedience to godly authority is critical and starts with the family, where obedience to parents is the training ground. On the other hand, it is clear from the Bible that ungodly authority must be resisted, and this needs discernment and wisdom.

5. **Leadership requires the articulation of a clear vision and mission.** God tells Moses to go to the "sons of Israel" to tell them that God had a plan to "bring them up out of the

affliction of Egypt ... to a land flowing with milk and honey" (Exodus 3:17). God is clear with Moses about His plan for Israel's deliverance. As God's chosen leader, Moses is given authority. God's authority given to Moses is made evident to human eyes through a staff that releases the power of God in miraculous ways. Moses also has support from his brother Aaron. When the elders of Israel first heard this message of deliverance, it must have seemed fanciful to them. They were told that God was arranging their release from captivity and that they would leave with great gifts bestowed by the Egyptians. However, Moses and Aaron had God's authority, and the message must have been articulated clearly and powerfully. The Bible says that when the elders of Israel heard the message, they "bowed their head and worshipped." Moses was able to present his mission to Pharaoh simply and clearly, with this request, "Thus says the Lord God of Israel: '**Let My people go** that they may hold a feast to Me in the wilderness.'"

Out of complexity comes simplicity, and leaders need to wrestle to define their vision and mission in a clear, simple, and precise way. "Let My people go" is an excellent example of a simple mission statement.

6. **Leaders always discover dissenters along the road, often those close to them and sometimes including their own family.** Moses had been given a mission from God Himself, and having led the Israelites out of Egypt, following many miraculous signs from which the Israelites had been spared, he must have thought that all would go smoothly. However, it wasn't long before there were murmurings and complaints among the people. Despite the mighty

work of deliverance, including the parting of the Red Sea for the Israelites to escape Pharaoh's troops, the children of Israel soon said to Moses: "Oh, that we had died by the hands of the LORD in the land of Egypt when we sat by the pots of meat and when we ate bread to the full! For you have brought us out into this wilderness to kill this whole assembly with hunger" (Exodus 16:3). These complaints did not cease even following God's miraculous provision of food and water. Even Moses' brother and sister made a stand against him. Incredibly, Moses' response in these situations was humility. When you receive criticism as a leader, you must consider that it could be correct. It is vital for leaders to evaluate criticism honestly and use it to check whether they are still on the right path. In these cases in the Bible, God Himself vindicated Moses, but at one point, when faced with the people's complaints yet again, Moses lashed out and disobeyed God, which changed his future. As a result of his behavior, due to anger, God prohibited Moses from entering the Promised Land.

7. **Leaders need to learn how to manage anger**. In the Book of Numbers, there is the strange story of when the children of Israel found themselves without water in the Wilderness of Zin at Kadesh (Numbers 20). It's a harsh location. Moses' sister dies here, and the Israelites cry out and complain again, saying, "Why did you bring us out here to die?" Moses, not unreasonably to our eyes after all he has brought them through, is angry with them and, in his anger, disobeys God by striking a rock to obtain water from it rather than speaking to the rock as God had instructed. This doesn't seem like a deal breaker to us, but it was a massive issue to

God. Moses is one of the greatest in the kingdom of God, but in his anger, he disobeyed God's instruction and struck the rock twice rather than speaking to it to obtain water. This disobedience, both personally and publicly, in his failure to honor the holiness of God before the people disqualified Moses and Aaron from entering the Promised Land. Anger is one of the most dangerous emotions for leaders because acting in anger can result in actions that, for the most part, are regretted later and can destroy people's trust. Leaders must learn to manage and work through their anger before they speak and act.

8. **Leaders need to delegate authority to others.** Leaders often have the sense that "only I can do it." Moses may have been in this category because he spent his days from dawn until dusk sorting out disputes amongst the people. His father-in-law Jethro, who was not an Israelite, saw this and realized that Moses' role was unsustainable. His advice to Moses was: "Moreover, you shall select from all the people able men, such as fear God, men of truth, hating covetousness; and place such over them to be rulers of thousands, rulers of hundreds, rulers of fifties, and rulers of tens. And let them judge the people at all times. Then it will be that every great matter they shall bring to you, but every small matter they themselves shall judge. So it will be easier for you, for they will bear the burden with you. If you do this thing, and God so commands you, then you will be able to endure, and all this people will also go to their place in peace" (Exodus 18:21–23).

Delegation is one of the biggest failures of leadership. Leaders find it difficult to delegate, but it can also be challenging to find "able men, such as fear God, men of truth, lacking covetousness."

Ultimately, success is determined by the people that leaders attract to them and to whom they delegate authority and responsibility. Moses appointed good men and gave them authority because they were men he could trust.

9. **Leaders must prepare carefully for the times they are absent.** At one point in the desert wanderings, God called Moses to meet him on Mount Sinai for 40 days and 40 nights (Exodus 24). On the mountain, God gave Moses detailed instructions for a special tent, a type of mobile temple, to be built where He would dwell amongst His people. These instructions last for many chapters of the Old Testament. Moses wasn't far away and was receiving instructions from God, but the elders of Israel thought that Moses may have gone forever—after all, six weeks is a long time to be away from your team when they have no idea about your plans. The elders came up with a terrible strategy to melt down all their jewelry and make a golden calf to worship and to which they could attribute their deliverance out of Egypt (Exodus 32:4). This idea had the support of Moses' brother Aaron, who chose fear of man rather than fear of God.

Idols come in many forms. One of the idols is the avalanche of social media and the "Twitter storm" that can arrive about some decision and distract leaders from their genuine leadership responsibility—to focus on their mission. Many leaders now also worship at the altar of "social justice" and various *causes du jour*, which have nothing to do with their company's mission but have the potential to divert the company away from its core purpose.

10. **Leaders must prepare successors**. Moses had a remarkable young man as an understudy who loved and feared God. Joshua, the son of Nun, "shadowed" Moses during his time in the wilderness. We discover that after the construction of the worship center (the tabernacle or tent of meeting), the Bible tells us that the Lord spoke to Moses as a friend. The Bible then adds that Moses "would return to the camp, but his servant Joshua the son of Nun, a young man, did not depart from the tabernacle" (Exodus 33:11). Joshua was a God-fearing man who sought the Lord and had the humility to be under authority. Moses prepared Joshua for the extraordinarily challenging task of leading the people of Israel into the Promised Land. After Moses' death, the Bible tells us that, "Now Joshua the son of Nun was full of the spirit of wisdom, for Moses had laid his hands on him; so the children of Israel heeded him, and did as the LORD had commanded Moses" (Deuteronomy 34:9).

Succession planning is not something that many organizations do well, but it is evident that Moses had prepared Joshua through the highs and lows of life in the desert. When it came time for Joshua to take over Moses' leadership, the children of Israel recognized his authority.

## Servant Leadership

Whether in the home, social settings, or at work, the ability to serve is the primary quality God seeks in a leader. Jesus had to deal with this issue in his followers when there was contention amongst his disciples about who would be the "top dog."

Jesus spoke to His disciples and the crowds that had gathered to hear Him saying:

*"He who is greatest among you shall be your servant. And whoever exalts himself will be humbled, and he who humbles* (in Greek—ταπεινόω transliterated as tapeinoō—to bring oneself low) *himself will be exalted"* (Matthew 23:11–12).

Jesus gave further understanding about leadership when the mother of two of His disciples, James and John, asked that her sons be given great authority (to sit on His right and left) in His kingdom. It's great to have a mother who wants her sons to go to the top! Jesus tells her that she doesn't know what she is asking. He replies:

*"You know that the rulers of the Gentiles lord it over them, and those who are great exercise authority over them. Yet it shall not be so among you; but* **whoever desires to become great among you, let him be your servant.** *And* **whoever desires to be first among you, let him be your slave**—*just as the Son of Man did not come to be served, but to serve, and to give His life a ransom for many"* (Matthew 20:25–28).

Surprisingly, Jesus tells us that outstanding leadership does not involve promoting oneself but being a servant. This is a hard lesson to learn and even harder to implement.

# Concluding Thoughts

Let's go back to the beginning of the chapter. Pat Murray asked two crucial questions about leadership. To answer his first question (**Who am I?**) requires intimate knowledge of yourself, including your strengths and weaknesses. I have covered some practical ideas for consideration in Chapter 3 concerning barriers to wisdom. If we are to demonstrate wisdom in leadership, it is essential to have self-understanding and awareness and to know our values and be prepared to stand on these.

Additionally, service must be our core value to succeed. Pat Murray's second question was, **what price am I prepared to pay**? Surprisingly, the price often is measured by how often you say no to opportunities that may seem exciting but may not be in your area of strength and calling and may compromise your values.

It is critical to be unflinching when asked to do something contrary to your core values. I recently spoke to a friend whose daughter worked for a large law firm, and she was asked to inflate her bill (which was already over $1 million) because her boss thought that the services were worth more to the client than the calculated billable hours. Despite being well-paid and liking her job, she resigned immediately rather than compromising her integrity. She was quite young but had already learned to hold the line on her "non-negotiables." Few will ever know what she did, but undoubtedly, it was the right decision. Learning to walk with personal integrity and upholding the non-negotiables in our lives is foundational to good leadership and good character.

## KEY POINTS ABOUT WISDOM IN LEADERSHIP

- **Everything rises and falls on leadership.**

- **Leadership involves having the heart of a servant**.

- **Good leaders must have an excellent understanding and awareness of themselves** and their values and be willing to pay the price to not compromise their integrity and non-negotiables.

- **Leaders must understand "the law of the lid"** and how their own capacity can limit the level at which their team can perform. Good leaders will develop strategies and processes to "lift the lid."

- **In leadership, it doesn't matter if the mission looks impossible if it has the backing of God.**

- **Past mistakes need not exclude us from leadership.**

- **A wilderness experience is often the ground of leadership preparation.**

- **Leadership involves obedience and submission to a higher authority**.

- **Leadership requires being able to articulate a clear vision and mission.**

- **Leaders always discover that there are dissenters along the road, often including those closest to them.**

- **Leaders need to learn how to manage their emotions, including anger.**

- **Leaders must take care and prepare for when they are absent, as others may compromise the core mission.**

- **Leaders need to be able to delegate authority and prepare successors.**

Our next chapter in the journey towards wisdom involves consideration of the importance of wisdom in love.

# CHAPTER 13
# WISDOM IN LOVE

*"We love Him because He first loved us." (1 John 4:19)*

Love is the most misunderstood word in the English language. Everyone has their ideas about love and what it means, but John, the disciple Jesus loved, provides the best insights about the origin and meaning of love.

## Principles About Love From John

John wrote a series of letters to the early church, and in his most extended letter (the First Letter of John), he wrote extensively about the centrality of love. As a disciple who knew Jesus personally and was close to Him when He walked the earth, John provides a shorthand summary of love for us:

"... God is love, and he who abides in love abides in God, and God in him" (1 John 4:16).

In this letter, John outlines a series of truths from God about love:

1. **The love of God in us is demonstrated by our actions—**keeping His commandments (1 John 2:3–6).

2. There is a **temptation for us to love the world** (which is passing away) rather than loving God and doing His will, which brings eternal life (1 John 2:15–17).

3. If we **practice righteousness and love our brother**, it demonstrates that we belong to God and that we know and love Him (1 John 3:10).

4. God shows His love for us by **sending his "only begotten Son"** into the world—(1 John 4:9).

5. **Love is known and demonstrated by Jesus laying down His life for us**; we likewise should lay down our lives for others. Love is known primarily by what a person does (1 John 3:16–18).

6. **Love one another** (for love is of God)—(1 John 4:7).

7. **Those who don't love don't know God**—(1 John 4:8).

8. There is **no fear in love,** but perfect love casts out fear—(1 John 4:18).

9. **God loved us first!** "We love Him because He first loved us"—(1 John 4:19).

John brings first-hand knowledge of God's love through his experience of Jesus' love. He writes intimately about this love because he was the "disciple whom Jesus loved" (John 19:26). Undoubtedly, he wasn't the only disciple that Jesus loved. However, there was indeed a special bond of love between them. John's direct experience of the love of the Father through Jesus was undeniably profound, and he wrote directly about love more than any of the other Bible writers.

Most of us, on hearing the word "love," think that it refers to a feeling. We all believe that we know what love is because we have had feelings of what we think is love at various times. However, love originates with God, and we need to know what He means when He speaks of love. We can't sideline God and think that we can understand and know what love is. So as we explore ancient wisdom in love, John is our best first-hand source, and he tells us that God is the origin of love and that God IS love.

## What Is Love?

The Bible tells us that God is love, and as we examine the descriptions of love throughout the Bible, we could say that love is an intention and commitment to put another person's welfare at the center of a relationship. In M. Scott Peck's excellent book *The Road Less Traveled*,[65] he defines love in this way: "The will to extend one's self for the purpose of nurturing one's own or another's spiritual growth." Scott Peck writes that love is primarily a choice as opposed to a feeling; it is a choice that involves effort, sacrifice, and the willingness to grow and change. However, while love is not defined as an emotion, love does result in a feeling of deep affection.

Let's look back to the ancient Hebrew writings in the Old Testament. We find that the word translated as "love" (אָהַב transliterated as *'āhaḇ*) is used over 200 times and is used to describe close relationships between parent and child or husband and wife. The word also is used to describe the relationship between God and the children of Israel. In the New Testament, several Greek words are translated into English as love. The two most common are *agapaō*, used for God's love or love for one another, and *philéo,* which has a meaning more along the lines of friendship. The Greek words are used interchangeably, but there are subtle differences that are too complex to explore here.

---

65  http://www.mscottpeck.com/

The amazing reality that the Bible teaches us about love is that it originates with God because God is love and that love will choose sacrifice or self-denial for the well-being of another. St Paul's famous writings about love in his First Letter to the Corinthians, which is often read at weddings, reveal various aspects of the complexity of love.

## Principles About Love From Paul

Most people in the West have heard the remarkable passage in Paul's First Letter to the Corinthian church. The letter indicates that this church was struggling to walk in God's ways, and it seems there was a lot of "fake love" in the church at that time. In this section of the letter, Paul points out that gifts such as oratory, prophecy, understanding of spiritual mysteries, faith even to move mountains, good works, feeding the poor, and self-sacrifice are nothing if love is not the foundation.

Paul writes:

"Love suffers long and is kind; love does not envy; love does not parade itself, is not arrogant; does not behave rudely, does not seek its own, is not provoked, keeps no accounts of evil; does not rejoice in iniquity, but rejoices in the truth; bears all things, believes all things, hopes all things, endures all things. Love never fails" (1 Corinthians 13:4–8).

In this section of his letter, Paul continues to write about various gifts and abilities that will eventually fail, but he declares that "love never fails." He finishes this passage on love by revealing that the spiritual virtues that will last forever are faith, hope, and love. He goes on to proclaim that the greatest of these is love.

If we think we are good at love, then we can test ourselves against Paul's list of what he describes love is and isn't. If we are honest, we will find that despite our best intentions, our nature is entirely consistent:

- We generally aren't prepared to suffer.

- We often can be unkind and envious of others.

- We like to "big note" and promote ourselves.

- We can be rude to others, even to our families.

- We generally seek our interests rather than the interests of others.

- When our "buttons are pushed," we can quickly become irritable or angry.

- We tend to hold grudges and unforgiveness against others, and in some cases, we can hold on to these for life.

- We are often easily offended.

- We can, at times, be secretly glad when something terrible happens to someone.

- We can become downcast from time to time and lose heart and hope.

As we examine this list and how we usually behave, it is easy to see how far from the reality of love we demonstrate daily. It's a good idea to have Paul's description of love somewhere handy, like on the refrigerator, so that we can look at it daily as an *aide memoire* to prompt us when we may be failing to meet the requirement of truly loving others.

Can we try harder to love? Well—we can, but failure is inevitable. What we need is a transformation from the inside out; this begins to become possible when we put our faith and hope in Jesus and the reality and power of His life in us. As mentioned in Chapter 11, this great mystery is written about remarkably by Watchman Nee, the Chinese Christian who stood against communism and inspired millions with his book *The Normal Christian Life*.[66] In essence, Nee tells us that it is not a matter of trying harder but drawing closer to and leaning upon God. This is not something that we can learn to do overnight, but God Himself will take us on the journey if we are willing. We indeed become like the people we spend time with. If we choose to seek God in His Word, the Bible, talk to Him, and intentionally be with Him in our daily lives, we will become increasingly changed to be like Him, and thus He will enable us to live as He does.

## Is the God of the Old Testament Vengeful and the God of the New Testament Loving?

In the early days of faith in God, I was confused about many difficult passages in the Old Testament. In the Old Testament, God seemed to smite many people, and He appeared to be an angry God. Jesus seemed less threatening. He was kind, healed many people, and was forgiving. I gravitated to the pages of the New Testament, where Jesus was kind to people and healed many. It took many years for me to understand that if, as the Bible says, God "is the same yesterday, and today and forever" (Hebrews 13:8), then I needed to come to an understanding of the more ancient Bible writings. I was fortunate to come across the teachings of Dr. Chuck Missler, the founder of Koinonia House, and his excellent series

---

66  https://www.amazon.com/Normal-Christian-Life-Watchman-Nee/dp/0875089909/ref=sr_1_3?crid=3BWOS7CYWTYP4&key-words=THe+normal+christian+life&qid=1675211774&sprefix=the+nor-mal+christian+lif%2Caps%2C346&sr=8-3

"Learn the Bible in 24 Hours." In these extensive teachings, Chuck said something simple that has helped me ever since in my study of the Bible: "The Old Testament is the New Testament concealed, and the New Testament is the Old Testament revealed."

Over time, I began to gain an understanding of the love of God revealed in the Old Testament. This was tough love to move the people He loved onto the right path. Today's Western societies, being deceived, have moved away from disciplining children to teach them right from wrong and healthy boundaries for life. This is not surprising as the West doesn't even acknowledge that good and evil exist, and we all want to do what is right in our own eyes.

However, in the Old Testament Book of Proverbs, King Solomon writes:

"He who spares his rod hates his son,

But he who loves him disciplines him promptly" (Proverbs 13:24).

God clearly teaches us in this verse that love requires discipline to teach right from wrong. This verse and others in Proverbs show that God, as a loving Father, disciplines His people for their good when He sees them going astray. Our modern culture is increasingly uncomfortable with the idea of punishment for evil and is even unwilling to admit that evil exists. However, God hates evil, and in Proverbs 6:16–18, some of these behaviors are outlined and give us an understanding of what evil looks like. God is holy (set apart) and so cannot tolerate evil but has to judge it. To our modern eyes, we cringe at the idea of God's judgment, which seems harsh and unforgiving. However, God moves at various times and places on the earth to judge evil and judged His own people Israel so that they would return to real life in Him. God will eventually return to destroy evil completely when Jesus returns to the earth to reclaim

His inheritance. In the meantime, God is longsuffering and gives us time to change our ways.

Undoubtedly, God is a God of judgment. However, He also is a God of love and mercy.

A significant verse in the Book of Exodus gives profound insight into God's character. It occurs when Moses went up to Mount Sinai and received the Ten Commandments. God said to Moses: "The LORD, the LORD God, **merciful and gracious, longsuffering, and abounding in goodness and truth, keeping mercy for thousands, forgiving iniquity and transgression and sin** ..." (Exodus 34:6). The mercy, lovingkindness, and longsuffering of God are reiterated throughout the Old Testament with similar ideas expressed in Numbers 14:18, Joel 2:13, Jonah 4:2, Nahum 1:3, Nehemiah 9:17, Psalm 103:8, and Micah 7:18.

Time and time again through the Old Testament, God demonstrated His care and compassion for His people, even though He often described them as "stiff-necked" because of their resistance to trusting and obeying Him. God repeatedly demonstrated His faithfulness to Israel, although they were unfaithful to Him. Despite being described as the least of all peoples, they are God's "special treasure" (Deuteronomy 7:6). This is outlined further in the next part of Deuteronomy: "The LORD did not set His love on you nor choose you because you were more in number than any other people, for you were the least of all peoples; but because the LORD loves you, and because He would keep the oath which He swore to your fathers, the LORD has brought you out with a mighty hand, and redeemed you from the house of bondage, from the hand of Pharaoh king of Egypt" (Deuteronomy 7:7–8).

God is the same God, a God of love, in both the Old and New Testaments. He also is a God who judges evil, and His ways are the ways of righteousness and justice. Living in a world with no hope for justice would be horrifying. God gives us ground for this hope because He will return to judge evil and restore justice. The Old Testament, in many places, provides a stark picture of judgment upon evil, which, as we've discussed, arises out of His love (for love and evil are incompatible). The New Testament provides a vivid picture of God's grace extended to humanity in Jesus Christ. However, God's judgment against evil is not absent in the New Testament. If we have eyes to see, it is clear that judgment was poured out upon Jesus on the cross for our sake. Jesus took the penalty for our wrongdoing that we may be forgiven.

In the Gospel of John, he describes, in a simple way, the difference in emphasis of the Old and New Testaments: "For the law was given through Moses, but grace and truth came through Jesus Christ" (John 1:17). The Law (which is holy and just) revealed human nature because we could not keep the law, and it revealed our incapacity to love. Woven through the Old Testament, God's grace shines despite human sin. However, in the New Testament, love came down and walked upon the earth in the person of Jesus, whom John tells us is God in the flesh (John 1:14).

Jesus came to reveal the Father in heaven and open another way for us, dependent not upon our capacity but God Himself. It is difficult to grasp the depths of love without knowing God and His commandments because God is love. Fortunately, God has helped us by giving us various gifts, such as marriage and friend-ships, and the relationships between parents and children, to help us experience and give love. He has also given us pets that, in extraordinary ways, teach us many things that reflect some of the elements of love we read about in 1 Corinthians 13.

# What I Learned About Love From My Dogs

As an only child who grew up in a remote part of Australia, dogs, cats, and ponies were my early and only companions. My dogs would accompany me on adventures to find rabbits, throw stones along the river, and play cowboys and Indians. As I grew up, I learned about sheepdogs and how to work with them to muster sheep and move them around the farm, and this helped me understand the unique capabilities of dogs. Much later, as a veterinarian, I treated many dogs and was constantly surprised at their trust in humans. In more recent years, two small poodle crosses, Snowy and Teddy, have joined our family in life on the farm. I am constantly fascinated by these wonderful companions and the incredible things they can teach us. Here are a few of my observations of dogs that provide insights into the story of love:

- **Dogs teach us about faith.** I hadn't fully considered this until my wife remarked that we frequently take the dogs on long car trips, and they always show delight about the travel. They jump into the car, having no idea where we are going, whether they will be in the car for five minutes or five days, and what we will do. However, they trust us and believe that whatever happens, it is going to be an adventure with something good in it for them. It is a beautiful insight into a life of faith in the one who cares for you. Dogs show faith daily by demonstrating that they believe in us to care for and provide for them. They show loyalty and devotion, though they do not know the future. They have no concerns, but they live by faith and know that what is coming will be good.

- **Dogs are loyal**. Sometimes people mistreat their dogs at times, but for the most part, dogs never seem to take offense, and they are always faithful and loyal. The story of Hachiko, the dog who waited at Tokyo's Shibuya train station every day for ten years in the hope that his dead master would return,[67] is an astounding depiction of unwavering loyalty. Humans have a lot to learn from dogs about loyalty.

- **Dogs are always delighted to see us**. When we return to the house after being outside, "Snowy," our small Schnauzer-Poodle cross, can see us coming back through a large, sliding glass door. When he was young, he decided to show his delight in seeing us by jumping two to three feet off the ground in a constant bounce until the door was opened. He continues to do this to this day, and his behavior, which appears to express great joy, has a remarkable impact on my wife and me and brings us great joy when we return to the house and "feel the love."

- **Dogs are forgiving**. Sometimes we can inadvertently mistreat dogs, or in some cases, this treatment is deliberate. Dogs never seem to hold a grudge. When our little dogs hit the wire on an electric fence designed for the horse enclosure, it never occurred to them that we were responsible for this terrible shock, and they came running to us for comfort. Fortunately, experience is a great teacher, and they haven't touched the fence again.

- **Dogs demonstrate their delight in being with us.** Dogs wag their tails in joy when they see us. They never seem to have a bad day but are always positive. We can learn a lot by following the lead of our dogs and being prepared

---

67  https://allthatsinteresting.com/hachiko-dog

to demonstrate our love more consistently to family and friends. Dogs show us unique expressions of unconditional love.

- **Dogs expect the best**. In reality, it seems that dogs are a type of high-class socialist. They have a handout mentality and never have to work for a living unless they are working dogs. Even working dogs seem to work with pleasure and delight. However, they are also grateful socialists and always seem to expect the best. Whether going for a walk, chasing kangaroos, or just waiting for their food, they anticipate that something good is coming their way at any moment.

## Some Thoughts on Wisdom in Romantic Love

King Solomon must have had more experience with romantic love than most, as 1 Kings 11:3 tells us that he had 700 wives who were princesses and 300 concubines. He also had a range of difficulties with his wives because while his Proverbs extol the blessings of a wife, he also wrote:

"Better to dwell in a corner of a housetop,

Than in a house shared with a contentious woman" (Proverbs 21:9).

Solomon understood the power of romantic love, and in the paean to love, the Song of Solomon (also called the Song of Songs), he wrote: "... love is as strong as death ... many waters cannot quench love, nor can floods drown it. If any man would give for love all the wealth of his house, it would be utterly despised" (Song of Songs 8:6–8). This description of love ascribes loyalty and power that will overcome any obstacle in its way. This love comes from another world and is entirely at odds with the modern Western understanding of love, which is often fickle, conditional, and self-centered at its core.

The New Testament writers wrote extensively about love, but the various translations are a little complicated because four Greek words are used to describe the one English word, love. Only two of these Greek words are used by the New Testament writers. One is *agapaō*, in essence, selfless, unconditional love, and the other is *philéō*, which is best translated as brotherly love or affection. The Greek word for romantic or sexual love is *eros* and is not used in the New Testament but appears in the Septuagint translation of the Old Testament that was written in the third century BC.

Romantic love or *eros* is powerful and one of the beautiful gifts of God but also one of the great dangers in life as it can easily be confused with lust. Some years ago, a woman in Sydney who was in love with a career criminal held in a maximum-security detention center hijacked a helicopter, forcing the pilot to land in the middle of a jail exercise compound to rescue the "love of her life."[68] She and her boyfriend spent six weeks on the run before they were reported to police by a suspicious trailer park owner. Both were recaptured and the woman, who had a previously unblemished record, spent seven years in prison. It is impossible to be sure what type of love motivated this woman to carry out such a high-risk raid on a prison. However, the story makes it clear that romantic love should be handled carefully, like a time bomb! Love is potent, and when you think of the danger and risk in the daring mission this young woman undertook to be with the man she loved, you realize that romantic love can completely overpower common sense and our understanding of right and wrong.

---

68  https://www.news.com.au/national/crime/devoted-girlfriends-daring-helicopter-prison-break/news-story/f73d686c4fd81541c1e1a-31b1a189149

No one understands all the factors that are involved in romantic attraction. However, it is possible to make some generalizations that depict some of the erroneous concepts in our culture about love: elite male sports stars are attracted to pretty blond women and vice-versa, sexual desire can override logical thinking, sexual desire is easily confused with love, "feelings" of love are difficult to sustain, and the attraction of opposites in personality often leads to long-term relationship difficulties because of innate difference. These are just a few examples, but God calls us to rise about the foolish notions of love and to learn to love as He does—a commitment to put others' welfare first.

I read Gary Chapman's helpful book, The Five Love Languages, some years ago.[69] Chapman writes that people receive love and have different love languages. As a result, there may be significant misunderstandings between spouses if they have different love languages. The five love languages that Chapman has noted are:

1.  Words of affirmation

2.  Quality time

3.  Receiving gifts

4.  Acts of service

5.  Physical touch

The love language concept is simple but significant. It is easy to see, for example, that if one spouse shows love by acts of service, and the other's love language is physical touch, there can be a disconnect where one or both people can feel unloved because they are not using the same love language. Chapman's book is

---

69  https://www.amazon.com/Love-Languages-Secret-That-Lasts/
dp/0802473156

highly recommended for all, as it is likely that we may not have recognized our spouse's love language. If so, our attempts to show them love may be unrecognized by them if we are not using their particular love language.

I have learned a little along the challenging road of romantic love, and here are my best ideas:

- **Communication** is the key to sustained romantic relationships but is one of the most challenging areas in which to excel. In general, men are not good listeners, especially after the early days of a relationship have passed. Most women need to be listened to and deeply understood rather than have their problems solved.

- **Forgiveness** is so crucial in romantic love that another way to spell love may be forgiveness. It is easiest to hurt the ones we love, and we need to be continually alert for the negative impact we may have had on our spouse and ready to seek forgiveness. St. Paul wrote quite simply: "... do not let the sun go down on your anger" (Ephesians 4:26, NASB).

- **Service** is an attitude that is critical to sustaining a romantic relationship. If you keep taking from the relationship, it is just like a bank account, and you will eventually become overdrawn and shut down. Relationships work best if, rather than looking for what we will get (we do this naturally), we look for what we can give.

- **Time** is another way of spelling love. Many relationships stumble and founder because other areas of life intrude and take precedence: children, work, friends, and family. It is easy to commit time in the early phases of a relationship, but this often becomes harder as time passes. For many women, quality time is a crucial love language, but all relationships need a commitment to time together in order to grow.

- **Valuing difference** is a challenge and an opportunity to grow in romantic relationships. Opposites tend to attract, but as time goes by, differences can be annoying and sometimes lead to relationship breakdown. It is important to celebrate differences and appreciate your partner's view, and consider this view carefully, mainly when it is different from your own when making significant decisions. It is also important to appreciate your spouse's diverse talents and skills because this is what makes the relationship stronger.

- **Appreciation** is one of the secrets to sustaining the fire of romantic love. Too often, the things you appreciate about the other person are taken for granted, and you fail to express the things you appreciate about them. Appreciation has an expiration date, so it is wise to make appreciation a daily habit.

- **Trust** is the foundation of all good relationships and even more so in romantic ones. We must grow in our capacity to be trustworthy and show that this is the case through our actions. A romantic relationship must be founded on mutual trust, and we must also take care to nurture this trust. Trust takes a long time to build but can be destroyed in just a moment.

## Conclusions

At the heart of love lies a mystery: love begins and ends with God, for God is love. We can't fully experience authentic love if we don't know God. Love is a choice and decision to act for the welfare of another and is self-sacrificing. It means to lay down our lives for another, either metaphorically and/or physically. God has given us various proxies for love to delight our senses and inspire us—love of beauty, nature, friends, spouses, and even pets. At the heart of love, these beautiful things in life are designed to teach us that God loves and cares for us and has our welfare as His highest aim, even if we sometimes find ourselves in difficult seasons of life. We can put our trust in God because God is love.

## KEY POINTS ABOUT WISDOM IN LOVE

- God is love, and we love because He first loved us. There is no love without God, and we need to understand God's love and ask Him to teach us His love.

- Love is a choice rather than just a feeling. Love is a decision and commitment to put another person's welfare at the center of a relationship and is sacrificial in nature.

- The God of the Old and New Testaments is the same God and is a God of love. We need to understand His character— His mercy, lovingkindness, righteousness, forgiveness, graciousness, longsuffering, and goodness, as well as His justice, His hatred of evil, and His judgment—if we are to understand love and begin to love God and what He loves.

- "Love suffers long and is kind; love does not envy; love does not parade itself, is not arrogant; does not behave rudely, does not seek its own, is not provoked, keeps no accounts of evil; does not rejoice in iniquity, but rejoices in the truth; bears all things, believes all things, hopes all things, endures all things" (1 Corinthians 13:4–8).

- Dogs can teach us much about love. From my dogs, I have learned about trust, faith, loyalty, forgiveness, expressing delight, and acceptance.

- Romantic love is powerful and delightful but also can be dangerous. Romantic love can be the foundation for much that is good on the earth through the establishment of families, God's central plank for achieving His purposes. Understanding your spouse's "love language" is crucial as you seek their welfare and the best way to love them well. I have found the following areas are important in romantic love: communication, forgiveness, service, time, valuing difference, appreciation, faithfulness, and trust.

Love is the greatest gift that God has given us. Of course, love has many faces, but one of the greatest and most challenging gifts that God has given us to teach us about love is marriage. Our next chapter in the journey of exploring ancient wisdom takes us into the joys and challenges of marriage.

# CHAPTER 14
## WISDOM IN MARRIAGE

*"Therefore a man shall leave his father and mother and be joined to his wife, and they shall become one flesh."*
*(Genesis 2:24)*

In my own experience of marriage, I am constantly learning and, hopefully, growing. Thus, I contend that it's impossible to be an expert on love and marriage because we are all a work in progress. However, it would have been interesting to have had Elizabeth Taylor's views after seven husbands and eight marriages (she married Richard Burton twice). She did say, "My troubles all started because I have a woman's body and a child's emotions,"[70] which is undoubtedly a bad foundation for a lasting marriage relationship.

In my parents' era, during the 1940s and 1950s, if a woman wasn't married by 21 years of age, she thought she was probably "on the shelf." My mother decreased her age by one year as she felt that at 25 years old, she could be too old to have a baby! Now, people are marrying later and often not at all. However, the modern ways do not seem to have created greater happiness but more emotional and mental health problems.

---

70  https://abcnews.go.com/Entertainment/marriages-liz-taylor/story?id=13202596

I have been married twice and have learned a lot along the way. When I first married in my 20s, I thought marriage would be easy. It's good to have great expectations for marriage, although, for the most part, these expectations are based on no actual knowledge. As the years went by, I realized that marriage was not easy, and the statistics across Western society bear this out: only 50% of marriages survive long-term. There is no evidence that we learn from our mistakes, as 67% of second marriages and 73% of third marriages end in divorce.[71]

Along life's journey of discovering more about marriage, I became chairman of a group of CEOs who were all high flying, well-remunerated, and smart. My job involved spending two hours with each of them every month as a coach. Gradually, I realized that apart from the usual stresses of their jobs, the more significant challenge was often their relationship with their spouse or partner. After doing this for a few years, I hypothesised that **everyone's marriage is in trouble, but most of us don't know it yet**. Marriage needs constant attention and nurture to prosper, and our instincts are often flawed. The hypothesis was backed up by many of the stories I heard and data from marriage counselors showing that most men are surprised when their wives leave them.[72]

I have put some effort into studying marriage because after my first wife died, I realized I had done an inadequate job as a husband. Fortunately, I had the opportunity to be married again. I began to understand that marriage was God's idea and that He had established marriage. God describes Himself as a husband

---

71  https://www.psychologytoday.com/us/blog/the-intelligent-divorce/201202/the-high-failure-rate-of-second-and-third-marriages

72  https://www.huffpost.com/entry/why-so-many-men-never-see_b_815502

to His people in several places in the Old Testament (Isaiah 54:5, Jeremiah 31:32, Hosea 2:16), and it is evident that marriage is something that has its origin in the heart of God and is sacred to Him and critical to His purposes. As a result of this awareness, I began to seek to understand more clearly His purposes and how to be a good husband.

I read dozens of books and sections of the Bible that dealt with marriage. Suddenly, I began to think I had become a marriage expert—it shows how easily we can deceive ourselves! My misguided sense of having some expertise relating to marriage was backed up when my wife and I were invited to go to Seychelles to speak about marriage in a series of talks to churches around the islands. However, in preparing for these talks, I realized how challenging it is to present the foundational essence of marriage, for at its heart, it is a mystery. Many years on, I am still growing in understanding of the ancient mystery of marriage. Simply, in this chapter, I will share some of the most important ideas I've learned.

## God's Plan for Marriage and the Family

God's plan at the beginning of time was for an intimate and lifelong relationship between a man and a woman. There is a remarkable and often overlooked passage in Genesis 2:21–22 where we are told that after Adam named all the animals:

" ... for Adam there was not found a helper comparable (or complementary) to him.

And the LORD God caused a deep sleep to fall on Adam, and he slept; and He took one of his ribs, and closed up the flesh in its place. Then the rib which the LORD God had taken from man He made into a woman, and He brought her to the man" (Genesis 2:20–22).

219

The Hebrew word in this passage that is translated as "helper" is עֵזֶר ('êzer), which means to help, support, or provide succor or sustenance.

The passage has several vital details that are essential to understanding God's plan for marriage:

- Adam was alone in creation, and God Himself intervened to create a "helper," someone who was complementary and not a challenger or competitor. Of course, this is not in line with modern thinking, but foundational principles forged into the fabric of creation itself don't change.

- Eve was physically created out of Adam in the first surgical operation in history. It is impossible for us with our modern scientific thinking to understand, but whether figurative or literal, the account tells us of the intimacy of God's creation of both man and woman. You can't get more intimate than a created helper formed from the rib of the first man. Adam's response was, "This, at last, is **bone of my bones and flesh of my flesh;** she shall be called Woman, because she was taken out of Man" (Genesis 2:23).

- God then proceeds to teach us: "Therefore a man shall leave his father and mother and be joined to his wife, and they shall become one flesh" (Genesis 2:24). This is an extraordinary revelation about God's purposes. Jesus reaffirms it by quoting the verse when asked by the Pharisees about divorce (Matthew 19:5). St. Paul also quotes the verse in Ephesians 5:31 in his teaching on marriage. The phrase is revelatory and contains vital information that I failed to understand in the early stages of marriage. God tells us that a husband is to leave his father and mother (physically and emotionally) as opposed to the wife leaving her parents. This is highly significant, radical, and often not understood. In marriage, the husband establishes a new allegiance and becomes "one flesh" with his wife.

In my first marriage, and as an only child, I did not understand this. In a sense, my parents had not released me, and I had not let go. I continued to have a strong emotional pull toward my parents, who frequently interfered with my relationship with my wife. Had I better understood the biblical proscription, I would have drawn more effective boundaries and saved my wife, myself, and our children from much heartache. In life, the central commitment of a husband is to his wife.

In later Bible writings, we are told that the "mystery" at the heart of marriage is profound and that the "two becoming one" is a signpost pointing us to the "mystery ... of Christ and the church" (Ephesians 5:32). It is easy for us Westerners to think of the church as a building, but in Greek, the church is the *ekklesia*, which is the called out ones. God's people are the ones who have heard the call to Himself. Marriage is not merely a legal or moral commitment but a remarkable spiritual mystery that God always designed to reflect and reveal the love that God has and desires for His people. Marriage tells us something quite profound about God's intention for the relationship He is establishing between His Son and His "called out ones." Indeed, the Bible tells us that at the culmination of all history is the wedding feast of Jesus and His bride, the church (Revelation 19:7–9). All weddings, intentionally or not, point to this incredible future event. God is calling all people to Himself in a relationship of love, and this will be fully realized in the age to come by those who hear His voice and respond.

So, from the beginning, God has had marriage at the center of His purpose and plan for humanity. Through the first man and woman, God purposed to populate the earth with children who would be made in His image, who would walk in friendship with Him and care for and steward His creation.

The underpinning of God's design has always been centered on the family, with the husband and wife providing complementary roles in raising children. The foundational unit for a cohesive and prosperous society is destroyed when the family is destroyed. Strong families (as defined by God) are foundational to the survival of a nation. Notably, when fathers are absent from homes, data show many adverse social outcomes:[73] feelings of abandonment, problems in attachment, child abuse, child obesity, crime and involvement with gangs, mental health problems, poor school performance, poverty, homelessness, and drug use.

Solid, stable marriages are the bedrock of a healthy, prosperous, and secure society and provide a way of refining us and teaching us more of God and His ways as we discover the delight and challenge of learning to love one another, and laying down our lives for each another. Our natural inclination for self-interest will soon be knocked out of us in the daily struggles of life together if a marriage is to last.

## Ancient Wisdom Regarding Marriage

Following on from embracing God's purposes in marriage, the choice of spouse is the next important factor regarding sustaining a lasting marriage. Interestingly, in ancient times, this process was

---

73  https://www.mnpsych.org/index.php%3Foption%3D-com_dailyplanetblog%26view%3Dentry%26category%3Dindus-try%2520news%26id%3D54

often one decided by parents, and Genesis 24 gives an extraordinary account of when Abraham sent his servant to seek out a wife for his son Isaac from amongst his relations in a distant land. Abraham demonstrates wholehearted faith in God and complete trust in his servant to find and bring back the right wife for his precious son Isaac, the son of Abraham's old age. God confirms the servant's identification of Rebekah as the wife for Isaac in the most marvellous but straightforward way after the servant prays to be led to God's choice for Isaac. Arranged marriages are still common in many parts of the world, including India, and have a high success rate. It is estimated that only approximately 1% of arranged marriages in India end in divorce.[74] The importance of seeking God for the right choice of a spouse cannot be overestimated because a wrong choice can bring a lifetime of pain.

The Book of Proverbs has much to say about the delights and dangers of marriage.

"An excellent wife is the crown of her husband, But she who causes shame is like rottenness in his bones." (Proverbs 12:4)

"He who finds a wife finds a good thing, And obtains favor from the LORD." (Proverbs 18:22)

"Houses and riches are an inheritance from fathers, But a prudent wife is from the LORD." (Proverbs 19:14)

On the other hand—things can go wrong as we are told:

"A foolish son is the ruin of his father, And the contentions of a wife are a continual dripping" (Proverbs 19:13).

---

74  https://www.psychologytoday.com/us/blog/the-science-behind-behavior/201511/why-are-so-many-indian-arranged-marriages-successful

Solomon, with 700 wives and 300 concubines, knew first-hand the experience of marriage difficulties as borne out in this proverb:

"Better to dwell in a corner of a housetop, Than in a house shared with a contentious wife" (Proverbs 21:9).

# Biblical Marriage Principles

What a challenge marriage is, yet it is the fundamental foundation of a stable, healthy, and prosperous society. You would think, over time, that the secrets to successful marriages might have become more evident. However, although there are various reasons, the divorce rate in the 1920s was only 1% compared to around 50% today. No wonder we are experiencing all kinds of problems nowadays in Western society. Yet we seem to be busy trying to fix the symptoms of family breakdown rather than understanding and supporting the foundations of marriage and family life.

I can't claim to be an expert on marriage, but I have learned some lessons over the past 50 years. It took me many years to grasp the heart of the Bible's wisdom concerning marriage, and I think I have finally begun to dimly see and apply these principles. The wisdom in the Bible concerning marriage increases the chance of success. Surprisingly, the secret is not more equality but recognizing and appreciating differences. Biblical wisdom acknowledges equality of the husband and wife but also appreciates differences. Here are a few of the fundamental principles that I have learned along the journey of married life:

### God Invented Marriage as a Life-long Commitment

When questioned about divorce by the Jewish religious leaders, Jesus made it very clear that marriage was a lifelong commitment between a man and a woman:

"Have you not read that He who made them at the beginning made them male and female, and said, 'For this reason, a man shall leave his father and mother and be joined to his wife, and the two shall become one flesh'? So then, they are no longer two but one flesh. Therefore what God has joined together, let not man separate" (Matthew 19:4–6).

Jesus told the religious leaders that God permitted divorce, beginning at the time of Moses, because He understood the hardness of men's hearts. However, God's purpose is that marriage be a lifelong commitment. In effect, we must shut ourselves and our spouse in jail together and then throw away the key! This is poorly understood in the modern world but was better understood 100 years ago at a time when the divorce rate was only 1%.

The great British Bible teacher Derek Prince taught in his book *The Marriage Covenant* that marriage is a binding agreement (covenant) between two people and made before God. The deal is not merely social or even legal but is, at its heart, spiritual, established by God to last a lifetime. Though we may not be aware of it, God has designed the marriage covenant with Himself at the center of the relationship. One of the beautiful descriptions of this is found in the Book of Ecclesiastes. The writer speaks of two people being better than one alone, and he finishes the section with the intriguing words, "... a cord of three strands is not easily broken" (Ecclesiastes 4:9–12). This verse refers to the strength of a plaited cord of three strands and symbolises the importance of weaving God, the author of marriage, into your relationship. Central to a happy and lasting marriage are the principles of forgiveness (see Chapter 7), which we need continuously in marriage and without which, a happy marriage is impossible.

## The Husband Leaves (Emotionally and Physically) His Parents

As discussed earlier in this chapter, biblical wisdom teaches us that it is the responsibility of a husband to leave his parents and establish a new family, where his wife's needs are pre-eminent (Genesis 2:24). The welfare of his wife is a husband's most significant concern. This does not come naturally to us husbands because we tend to be principally focused on our own needs.

## Husbands Need to Lay Down Their Lives for Their Wives

As outlined earlier in the chapter, God's wisdom teaches us that the relationship between a husband and wife, in some inexplicable way, is designed to reflect the reality of the relationship between Christ and the church. Jesus is the example given to us. He willingly laid down His life for the church. St. Paul tells husbands to: "Love your wives, just as Christ also loved the church and gave Himself for her" (Ephesians 5:25). This is an impossible requirement for husbands without God's help. Still, it speaks to the high calling of being a husband and the primacy of seeking the wife's welfare at all times. This is the mysterious and, without God's help, impossible but central calling of being a husband. A husband's role in marriage is sacrificial, focused on his wife's welfare. Practically, this means being the first to say sorry, to seek your wife's welfare before your own and to consider your wife's needs in making decisions. Also, it means really knowing and understanding your wife so that she prospers emotionally, physically, and spiritually. The former U.S. president, Lyndon B. Johnson, may have understood something of this challenge when he is reported to have said: "I have learned that only two things are necessary to keep one's wife happy. First, let her think she's having her own way. And second, let her have it."[75] More seriously, Derek Prince was once asked about the nature and character of a certain man. He replied, "I don't know yet; I haven't met his wife yet."[76] This insightful statement throws great illumination on the role of a husband and his part in his wife's welfare and well-being (security, esteem, joy, confidence, peace, etc.).

## The Husband Is the Head of the Wife (As Christ Is the Head of the Church), and the Wife Should Submit to the Husband

St. Paul writes, regarding relationships, "... submitting to one another in the fear of God. Wives, submit to your own husbands, as to the Lord. For the husband is head of the wife, as also Christ is head of the church; and He is the Savior of the body" (Ephesians 5:2123). This sounds ridiculous to modern ears, but it is a foundational principle of wisdom for marriage. The radical precept to our current way of thinking is that the wife is called to submit to her husband, who loves her as Christ loved the church and is laying down His life for her. Submission is not something the husband demands but that the wife freely gives to the one laying down his life for her. The radical idea at the heart of Jesus' teaching is that headship means being a servant (Matthew 23:11–12). Furthermore, the Bible says that Jesus, who is God and head of the church, "... existing in the form of God, counted not the being on an equality with God a thing to be grasped, but emptied himself, taking the form of a servant" (Philippians 2:6–7). Providing instruction for wives, Paul says to "respect their husbands" (Ephesians 5:33). This seems to be challenging for wives because I think they suspect that their husbands are idiots, and they may well be correct.

---

75  https://libquotes.com/lyndon-b-johnson/quote/lbz5y0m
76  https://www.derekprince.com/teaching/07-2

Nonetheless, wisdom dictates that a wife respects her husband and submits to him. She is secure in knowing that her husband is seeking her welfare and is prepared to lay down his life. Of course, these ideas can seem like strange fiction to modern ears, but when husbands and wives understand their differing roles and responsibilities and act on them, it is a recipe for marital harmony, strength, and joy.

If a husband seeks his wife's highest welfare and gives her loving security, then submission and respect will likely follow. These are ancient, timeless principles. However, the submission of wives to husbands, together with respect by wives for their husbands, is counter-cultural. Of course, a husband can't demand submission or respect, but undoubtedly, if your wife sees you laying down your life for her in love, she will be more likely to respect you and submit to your leadership. A husband should not be concerned about seeking his wife's submission and respect—that is something between the wife and God. The husband should simply say on his side of the equation to love his wife as Christ loved the church.

It is essential to add that in Ephesians 5:21, there is a direction to all God's people to "submit to one another." This emphasizes the mutual respect and humility to be exercised among God's people. Of course, it is important for husbands and wives to explore and discuss life's issues and arrive at a joint decision. However, if an agreement can't be reached, the husband is called by God to take responsibility for the decision (taking account of the wife's greatest welfare), and the wife is called to submit and trust both God and her husband.

Undoubtedly, marriage, as the most critical unit for God's plan, is under increasing attack. It's sometimes hard for us to realize the severity of the attack in the day-to-day challenges of life. I read an excellent book on marriage many years ago by John and Stasi Eldredge,[77] and a memorable line that stayed with me was, "In marriage, you have an enemy, and it's not your spouse!" Satan is the fierce enemy of marriage, and it is good to remember this simple line when you are angry with your spouse. The integrity and strength of marriage (and, therefore, the family) is one of the central planks of God's purposes on the earth. The level of spiritual attack waged against marriage is not surprising. The Bible tells us that in the last days, when evil is reaching a peak, marriage will be banned (1 Timothy 4:3). In the meantime, we see world rulers re-defining and expanding the definition of marriage. Standing in and for God's truth in marriage is not for the faint-hearted, but it is the only way for those who understand it is the truth.

## Some Important Ideas to Consider When Choosing a Life Partner

If marriage is a lifelong decision, we had better get it right! Unfortunately, even among Christians, most do not have the concept of marriage as a lifelong commitment. Data from large companies show that most employee hiring decisions have a 50:50 chance of success. The current divorce figures show a similar long-term success rate for marriage. So—in both the areas of hiring employees and marriage, you can flip a coin and achieve current outcomes. To have a lasting marriage relationship, making a sober, considered, and prayerful decision in choosing a marriage partner is crucial. As King Solomon points out, it is: "Better to dwell in the wilderness, than with a contentious and angry woman" (Proverbs 21:19). While this is written regarding a woman, we can apply the same idea to men.

---

77  https://www.christianbook.com/love-finding-marriage-youve-dreamed-ebook/john-eldredge/9780307590237/pd/11573EB

How do you make a good decision? Fortunately, the Bible has much to say about this, and Derek Prince has collated much of this in a small booklet called "The Choice of a Partner."[78] Another book with outstanding material about marriage is titled *God Is a Matchmaker*.[79] Following are a few of Derek's fundamental principles that help us consider the choice of a marriage partner. Also, I have added some of the wisdom I've learned.

## Marriage Is Designed by God

As we have already discussed, it is God who designed and planned marriage, and so it is wise to seek God to provide a life partner. God's design and purpose in marriage are evident in the early pages of the Bible (Genesis 2:24) and at the conclusion (Revelation 19:6–9). The Bible essentially begins and ends with a marriage. Additionally, God tells us that "... a prudent wife is from the LORD" (Proverbs 19:14). Marriage is God's idea, and He desires to be deeply invested in marriage as the third strengthening strand. If we ask Him, we can trust Him to bring us a life partner with whom we can grow and flourish.

## Choosing a Marriage Partner Is One of the Most Important Life Decisions

Firstly, a Christian should never select a non-Christian partner (see Amos 3:3 and 2 Corinthians 6:14–18). Derek tells a story (page 45) in his short booklet[80] that Charles Spurgeon initially told: "A young lady once took a young man to see her pastor and said: 'This is the young man whom I am going to marry.' 'Is he a Christian?'

---

78  https://www.ministryhelps.com/the-choice-of-partner-derek-prince-p-3221.html

79  https://www.derekprince.com/books/god-is-a-matchmaker

80  https://www.ministryhelps.com/the-choice-of-partner-derek-prince-p-3221.html

asked the pastor. 'Not yet,' said the young lady, 'but I will help him to become one after we are married.' 'Before you finally make up your mind, I would like you to do something for me,' said the pastor. He pointed to a table in the room and said, 'Just climb up unto that table and stand there for a moment.' The young lady did so. 'Now,' said the pastor, 'give the young man your hand and try to lift him up onto the table beside you.' Then he turned to the young man and said, 'Now you try to pull the young lady down to you.' Within a few moments, the young lady was down on the floor beside the young man! 'That's how it will be when you are married,' said the pastor. 'You will not be able to pull him up to your level, but he will pull you down to his!' So it is when a Christian marries an unbeliever. It is always easier for the non-Christian partner to make the Christian a backslider than for the saved partner to make the unbeliever a Christian."

## "Above All, Guard Your Heart, for It Is the Wellspring of Life" (Proverbs 4:23)

Derek Prince's insight is: "In our contemporary culture, young people, in particular, are being bombarded continually with influences that undermine biblical standards for sex and marriage. These are at work through teaching in schools and colleges, through the media, through peer pressure, and through other ways that are hard to detect. **If you are to find God's plan for marriage in your life, you must set a guard over your heart ...**"[81]

We live in a culture where there is no guarding of the heart by young people, and it has become the norm even to send intimate photographs to potential suitors. A "hook-up" culture has emerged, propelled by internet dating sites, and the floodgates

---

81  https://www.derekprince.com/books/god-is-a-matchmaker

have been opened to emotional and spiritual disaster. In ancient times, great care was taken to ensure that young women's hearts were protected, but the women's rights movement has resulted in any guardrails being completely removed. Guarding your heart is critical to avoid the emotional pain and subsequent mental health issues that can result from opening your heart without discernment.

## Be Prepared to Trust God and Wait

This is a critical piece of advice but the most challenging to follow. Rather than finding "Mr. or Mrs. Right," I often have seen situations when people settle for "Mr. or Mrs. Right for Now"—and longevity in marriage is unlikely to result. When you marry "Mr. or Mrs. Right for Now," often because of desperation, it won't be long before your misgivings surface and the marriage ends. Waiting is difficult in seeking to find the right one, but it is always worthwhile. An important Bible verse is from Isaiah 64:4—"for since the beginning of the world, men have not heard nor perceived by the ear, nor has the eye seen any God besides You, who acts for the one who waits for Him."

## Character Is Critical

Character should be noted carefully. Derek says, "Marriage does not change a person's character. If a person has a bad character before marriage, that person will still have a bad character after marriage."[82] Look for things such as: are they easily provoked to anger, does the person lie to excuse themself, are they miserly or generous, how do they relate to your family and friends, and are they reliable? Look for crucial character traits such as humility, pride,

---

82  https://www.ministryhelps.com/the-choice-of-partner-derek-prince-p-3221.html

integrity, addictions, kindness, harshness, diligence, constancy, self-control, self-awareness, ability to accept negative feedback, and capacity for forgiveness. Many of these character traits result from innate personality and family upbringing. I have observed that women, in particular, believe in their ability to change a man but are invariably wrong. When approaching marriage, you need to understand that you are likely to be living with a person whose character remains unchanged despite your best efforts. The most important question is: can I live with the disagreeable parts of my potential spouse's personality for the rest of my life?

## Seek Counsel

Proverbs 12:15 says, "The way of a fool is right in his own eyes, but he who heeds counsel is wise." Counsel from parents and family members regarding the choice of a marriage partner is essential, especially when negative. Unfortunately, this advice often is ignored. The most challenging advice to consider is advice we don't want to hear (and act on) but may be correct. Be careful to listen to negative feedback about your future spouse. Sometimes, it may be ill-founded, but those closest to you may often notice things that you may be blinded to when you are in thrall to love.

## Opposites Attract—But This May Be a Hidden Relationship Time Bomb

It is interesting how often we are attracted to a person who is opposite in character and temperament. Psychologists explain this phenomenon as people unconsciously looking for "completeness." In most of my observations, an introvert will be attracted to an extrovert and vice-versa; a person with an eye for detail will be attracted to a big-picture thinker; a messy person will be attracted to a tidy person, etc. These differences often bring great joy but, in the longer term, may cause significant difficulties because, eventually, the differences irritate and cause conflict. The person who is the life of the party finds that their partner wants to stay home and read. Conflict can then ensue. It is essential to learn to recognize the combined strength in complementary differences. Therefore, it is essential to understand what strengthens your partner and to take time to ensure that you prioritize the things that bring them life, joy, and strength. As the French say—"*Vive la différence!*"

## A Roving Eye Will Lead to Disaster!

The evil and destructive impact of adultery is downplayed and hardly recognized as an issue in today's society, which the idea of "no-fault divorce" has supported. Many warnings about the devastating nature of infidelity are woven throughout the Book of Proverbs. Here is one such particular warning:

> "Whoever commits adultery with a woman lacks understanding; He who does so destroys his own soul Wounds and dishonor he will get, And his reproach will not be wiped away. For jealousy is a husband's fury; Therefore he will not spare in the day of vengeance" (Proverbs 6:32–34).

# Conclusions: Marriage Has Its Origins in the Heart of God: It Belongs to Him

There is no doubt that marriage is one of life's greatest delights and joys but also one of the most significant challenges. God's ancient wisdom in unfolding marriage starts at the beginning of time in the creation story. Marriage belongs to God, and we can anticipate His support when we seek Him and His ways in marriage. I liked this quote that is unattributed but captures the wonder of marriage:

"Marriage is like setting sail; it's an adventure with endless possibilities and uncharted waters. But the secret to a successful voyage is to trust your partner, weather the storms together, and always keep your love as your anchor" (Anon.).

# KEY POINTS ABOUT WISDOM IN MARRIAGE

- It is salutary to remember the observation that "everyone's marriage is in trouble; it's just that most of us don't know it yet."

- God saw that it was not good for man to be alone, and His plan from the beginning was to create a helper for man comparable to him. God created woman, someone who was complementary to man and not a competitor or challenger.

- God's design in marriage was for a "man to leave his mother and father and be joined to his wife, and they shall become one flesh" (Genesis 2:24).

- There is a great mystery in marriage, and God describes the union of a man and woman in marriage as comparable to the mystical union of Christ and His church (Ephesians 5:32).

- Solid and stable marriages are the bedrock of societies and nations.

- Marriage provides a way of refining us and teaching us God's ways as we discover the delights and challenges of laying down our lives for one another in marriage.

- The ancient wisdom of the Bible provides countercultural advice about success in marriage:

  - When they get married, husbands need to learn to put their wife's needs and the needs of their new family first.

- The new husband must leave his parents to establish a new family with his wife. The husband is responsible for leaving his parents, physically and emotionally, and building a new family.

- A husband is responsible for nurturing and encouraging his wife. Her well-being is his highest responsibility under God. Husbands are called to lay down their lives for their wives, just as Jesus did for the church.

- Wives should submit to their husbands and respect them.

- Marriage is a covenant: a binding and unbreakable physical and spiritual agreement between a man and a woman before God. Furthermore, the image of a cord of three strands (Ecclesiastes 4:12), with God as the third strengthening strand, is important because God is woven into marriage and will help us when we seek Him.

- It is essential to consider many issues when choosing a marriage partner. These include: seeking God for His choice, carefully examining character, guarding your heart, seeking wise counsel, and being prepared to wait.

- While opposites attract, there can be a hidden challenge down the road because of the need to understand differences.

- Remember—you have an enemy, and it's not your spouse. It's the great deceiver! Because opposites attract, it is easy to find yourself in conflict with your spouse, but you need to learn and appreciate differences.

- Choosing a marriage partner is one of the most important decisions we make in life and should be taken carefully and with regard to what you know about the potential spouse's character and with counsel from close family and friends.

- Adultery devastates marriages and is one of the most common causes of marriage breakdown. A roving eye leads to destruction and death. No one is immune, and we need to guard our hearts.

We are nearing the end of our journey into ancient wisdom for modern times. Let's move on to the next chapter and consider ancient wisdom from the Bible about parenting. Undoubtedly, parenting is one of life's most demanding and rewarding tasks, and mistakes are easy to make. It is easy to become an expert in how to deal with **other** people's children!

# CHAPTER 15
# WISDOM IN PARENTING

*"Honor your father and your mother, that your days may be*
*long upon the land which the LORD your God is giving you."*
*(Exodus 20:12)*

Nothing will create more trouble within families than sharing ideas and advice about parenting. Grandparents often have a conflict with their own children when they take responsibility for their grandchildren's care (which includes discipline) when they come to stay. In contemporary culture, it's not unusual that grandparents think their grandchildren lack discipline, and it seems wise to pull them back into line. After the visit, the parents may be offered "free" advice. This can end in family conflict and even division, so we need to recognize that we are entering complex territory when we are involved in the care of children. It is easy to be blindsided by trouble we didn't anticipate when it comes to ideas about parenting, which often can differ between husband and wife.

Amazingly, without instruction or experience, it is easy to think of ourselves as "experts" before we have even had children or had experience in child care. At least—this is what I thought, and I have discovered that most of us feel the same way—everyone thinks they are an expert.

I remember speaking to a prominent Archbishop of the Anglican Church in Australia who said that after his first two children, he and his wife were so impressed with their parenting skills that they considered writing a book. However, they then had challenging twins, and everything they thought they knew about parenting was thrown out the window. They began to feel like parenting failures, and all their ideas about parenting were consigned to the trash can! They had been beaten by the clever twins, who had conspired against them, and the parents realized that they needed to return to the parenting drawing board.

Being a parent is a great leveler, and after more than 40 years of being a parent, I can claim that I know nothing, but I can see my mistakes more clearly. The problem is that our instincts are frequently wrong, and we must remember that the great danger in modern times is not being too firm. Instead, we enter negotiations with children on the basis of logic and a sense that they love us and want to do what we suggest. However, it would usually be wiser to imagine that we are negotiating with terrorists, who have a "take no prisoners" approach and negotiate accordingly.

Ancient biblical wisdom is timeless; some foundational concepts about raising children are the following.[83]

## Parenting Is More About Teaching Right Relationships Than Just Teaching Right Behavior

Within a family, children quickly see themselves as equals (or superiors) in a struggle for supremacy. You can see this struggle at

---

83  https://ca.thegospelcoalition.org/columns/ad-fontes/10-parent-ing-imperatives-book-proverbs/

any supermarket checkout with a parent and child "negotiating" about the child's perceived need for more candy. It is evident that the child has the upper hand in any "negotiation." Mostly, we are unprepared for this battle, and the combination of weariness and previous capitulation make us ripe to become the victims of "Stockholm Syndrome."[84] Like Patty Hearst, we can find ourselves trapped by our "captors" and obediently doing what they tell us.

I often ask my Sunday School class, "Did anyone have to teach you to be naughty?" They all say, "No. We learned it ourselves!" It is a good way of understanding that we are all born with a capability for sin and wrongdoing and need to learn correction. This understanding is an excellent way to introduce the reality that God is the boss of everything. He has instituted order in the family, with a foundation of "the fear of the Lord" (Proverbs 1:7) for the care and well-being of everyone in the family.

Parents are responsible, under God, for raising their children in the "fear of the Lord." Just as we all need to fear God, we must respect His delegated authority to parents. Parents are responsible to God for their parenting and need to act wisely and consistently in carrying out their God-given role. The fifth of the ten commandments says, "Honor your father and mother, and you will live a long life in the land that the Lord your God has given you" (Exodus 20:12). Dishonor is not a word that is much used today, and even the word honor is all but lost from our vocabulary. However, honor means to respect, esteem, defer to, and also, in the case of parents, obey. Dishonor to parents needs to be addressed quickly and decisively as, at its heart, it is the dishonor of God.

---

84 https://my.clevelandclinic.org/health/diseases/22387-stockholm-syndrome

Children must understand that there is a hierarchy of order in the family and that they are not living in a socialist utopia where everyone is equal. Many of us make the mistake of reasoning with our children as though we could persuade them that our view is correct. If we get into the battle of ideas with our children, we have already lost! The central concept we need to teach our children is something along the lines of the following: "I am responsible to God for teaching you His ways. His ways are good for you and the whole family. I love you, and even if you don't understand what I tell you now, you must accept it because if you don't, you are rebelling against God and me. If you disobey and rebel against us, your parents, you are choosing a way that is bad for you."

Of course, this type of discussion has to be age-appropriate, and with increasing age comes increasing independence. However, the teenage years are often the most difficult because this is when children still need clear boundaries that are well-enforced to grow into emotionally healthy adults. Usually, teenagers rebel against the authority of their parents, and it needs real wisdom to know how to respond in any given situation. It is good to remember, though, that you could be negotiating with cunning terrorists!

Even as I write this, I realize that talking like this to children sounds outlandish to modern ears. Nonetheless, it is God's wisdom and is a pathway to life and freedom. To go down the other road and let children call all the shots through disobedience and simply wearing us down is a road that leads to spiritual and emotional wreckage for all.

# Teach and Give Precedence to God's Word in the Bible

If we are to teach right relationships to children (as foundational to family life), then from an early age, children need to be taught the basics of God's Word in the Bible. The Book of Proverbs tells us that,

"For the LORD gives wisdom; From His mouth come knowledge and understanding;" (Proverbs 2:6)

and

"Whoever despises the word brings destruction on himself, but he who reveres the commandment will be rewarded" (Proverbs 13:13).

According to biblical wisdom, parents are responsible and accountable to God. As such, His Word is the ultimate authority in family life. God tells us to teach our children His commandments and His ways, which are increasingly at odds with society's current norms. If we have the proper foundation in God's wisdom and commandments, then when we make a decision, we need to do as Jesus said: "But let your 'Yes' be 'Yes,' and your 'No,' 'No.' For whatever is more than these is from the evil one" (Matthew 5:37).

Unfortunately, many of us do very poorly in saying no. Our no often sounds like a "maybe"! Almost every parent has been caught in a pincer movement by a cunning child, who, having obtained a "no" from one parent, goes to the other to try a new angle and turn the decision around. The two foundational rules for parents are **solidarity** and **consistency**. No matter what happens, parents need to act in unity and consistently. Often this is difficult and increasingly so when there are split households.

One thing I've noticed is that the two parents often come from families with very different norms. This can remain unknown to them until there is a crisis, such as the arrival of a child. It is critical that, before the crisis, the two parents agree on what is foundational to family life and what will be their "family norms" together. This enables parents to act in unity with consistency and not to be divided. As discussed earlier, it is easy to find ourselves entering into a "negotiation" with a child, where we are sure to lose rather than just reinforcing the agreed rule and not deviating from it.

## Be Thankful for and Appreciate Correction

Correction or chastening is always challenging for parents Something in our inner being rejects correction. However, correction for children is a foundational principle taught throughout the Bible. The Book of Proverbs has much wisdom in this area:

"My son, do not despise the chastening of the Lord, Nor detest His correction; For whom the Lord loves He corrects, Just as a father the son in whom he delights" (Proverbs 3:11–12).

Children must learn to understand that correction is a sign of love. It is the sign of a parent who cares and is willing to take the time to teach their children for their welfare. God says that when He corrects or chastens us, it is a sign of His love for us. Most of us hate discipline, and the typical response of most children is to sulk and show a bad attitude. This is something that parents cannot tolerate, as it is a quality that will pursue us all our lives and, if unaddressed, will have a negative impact on character. An old saying I like is that "Your attitude determines your altitude." How far and high you go in life often is a direct outcome of your attitude, which is ultimately connected to character. A negative manner, sense of victimhood, underlying anger, or other such symptoms reveal an attitude that says—"I demand to be given more in my life." If this attitude is not corrected and becomes embedded in a child's character, there will be adverse outcomes in life, love, and work.

In families, in workplaces, and with friends—openness to correction is a sign of maturity and Godly wisdom.

In a similar vein, Proverbs 12:1 tells us: "Whoever loves instruction loves knowledge, But he who hates correction is stupid."

We must all learn to walk in humility and love instruction and correction. This quality can be nurtured in our children as we teach them to listen and receive instruction and correction from an early age. This character quality is much harder for an older person to learn if they were not taught as a child. However, nothing is impossible with God!

This brings me to the critical role of how to discipline. The Book of Proverbs tells us:

"He who spares his rod hates his son, But he who loves him disciplines him promptly" (13:24).

This idea is reiterated in Proverbs 22:15—"Foolishness is bound up in the heart of a child; The rod of correction will drive it far from him."

And also, Proverbs 29:15:

"The rod and rebuke give wisdom, But a child left to himself brings shame to his mother."

Now, I am not suggesting that Proverbs is just a simple child-raising handbook, but it is true that "sparing the rod" may not be a sign of care and love for the child but, surprisingly, may indicate hatred (or at least, fear). According to the verses above, it seems that judiciously and appropriately applying "the rod" may set a child on a path away from foolishness, shame, and even hell.

There was a time (certainly when I was growing up) when the "rod of correction" was widely used by parents—probably some parents applying this technique well and others injudiciously. I know that "modern wisdom," which eschews "applying the rod," is not giving outstanding results in child raising but a generation glued to electronic devices and frequently disrespectful, disobedient, antisocial, and aggressive.

The Book of Proverbs has many verses about the importance of correcting children, and we are told:

"Train up a child in the way he should go, And when he is old, he will not depart from it" (Proverbs 22:6).

However, there is a dark side to correction, and one sees this daily with terrible child abuse cases. Discipline must be given carefully and wisely so that the punishment meets the crime. St. Paul understood this when he wrote: "Fathers, do not provoke your children, lest they become discouraged" (Colossians 3:21), and, "Fathers, do not provoke (exasperate) your children to anger by the way you treat them. Rather, bring them up with the discipline and instruction that comes from the Lord" (Ephesians 6:4 NLT).

I was an only child who grew up in the country without the experience of seeing other children being disciplined. However, my mother wasn't at risk of "sparing the rod"! One of my later memories from my 20s was when I was living in an apartment in the city next to a house where there were many children, often yelling and arguing in the backyard. Intermittently, I would hear the mother come out into the backyard and scream above the noise, "Youse kids, shut up, or I'll kill youse all!"

Even at that stage of my life, without any experience with children, I could discern that when your top and only discipline technique is to threaten death but never carry out your threats, results will be poor. Also, despite my lack of experience, I realized there had to be something more appropriate and intermediate between screaming and threatening death!

I'm pleased to report that I did learn something—and as far as I can remember, I never threatened my children with death. Probably being afflicted with the mood of the age, I may have spared the rod too much when my children were growing up. This is a difficult balance to get right, but I know that the biblical wisdom of King Solomon concerning "the rod" comes from God.

## Honor Your Father and Mother

It is impossible to consider ancient wisdom without considering the Ten Commandments God gave Moses. Of the commandments, the only commandment that comes with a reward for obedience is Commandment Five: "Honor your father and your mother, that your days may be long in the land that the Lord your God is giving you" (Exodus 20:12). The Hebrew word for honor is כָּ בֵ ד translit-erated as kābad and implies heaviness, weightiness, or seriousness. Honoring your father and mother is a weighty responsibility, and as discussed earlier, it means that you respect them, listen to them, and seriously consider their advice. It also involves caring for them, considering their needs, and loving them, notably in their older age. For younger children, who are still dependent, it means to respect, listen, and obey.

Solomon follows up on God's commandment regarding parents in the early part of Proverbs and says (Proverbs 1:8–9):

"My son, **hear the instruction of your father**, And **do not forsake the law of your mother**; For they will be a graceful ornament on your head, And chains about your neck."

God created the family as the cornerstone of society and the foundation of a nation. Among God's ten commandments, given to Moses when the children of Israel were on their long desert journey, the necessity of honoring your father and mother is, to we Westerners, a surprising commandment. It comes immediately after the first four commandments relating to God's centrality and to true worship. Most people don't even know this commandment about honoring your parents, but if they do, they fail. God says honoring your father and mother brings the reward of "long life in the land that God is giving you" (Exodus 20:12). It is reasonable to deduce that the corollary (i.e., failure to honor parents) is likely to lead to a shorter life in the land. I have written in detail about my experience of trying to honor my father and mother in Chapter 1, and readers may find it helpful to review this section.

Today in society, a family with a mother and father living together is a rarity. Parenting is challenging and stretches us to our limits. I greatly admire single parents who take on and manage this demanding role. The role of a parent is one of inestimable importance to instruct children carefully and help them grow into understanding "the fear of the Lord." God's design was that "a father's instruction" and obedience to the "law of the mother" (Proverbs 1:8), when heeded by the child, be like an adornment through the forging of character that would grace the child's life all their days.

# Take Time to Understand and Affirm Your Child

It is vital to grow in understanding who our children are and not just treat them as an image of ourselves or seek to have them fulfil our dreams. The secret lies in taking the time to understand and know the child's heart—what brings life and strength to them in their daily life, what brings fear, what they enjoy, and what leaves them feeling despondent. This takes time and patience because every child is different, with distinctive strengths and challenges, and a one-size-fits-all policy will not work. Children are also very sensitive to injustice, so it is essential not to provoke them, and fathers need to be aware of this. Nonetheless, suppose fathers will make it a priority to take the time to build foundations, especially in the early years with their children, and are just and fair in their application of boundaries and discipline. In that case, there is less likelihood of rebellion in the later years.

I saw this recently with a father whose son had begun work as a trainee carpenter for a small building business. The business owner was inspirational but lacked good organizational skills or any business systems. Many people had resigned from the company because of the disorganization. However, the young man's father who worked in the building industry himself, told his son: "Don't leave the business owner while the owner is in difficulties with many people leaving. Complete your time there by working through until the end of the year. Then you will have fulfilled your obligation, and you will be able to leave with the support of your boss, who will understand your need to gain further training elsewhere."

It was wise advice, and the teenage son heeded his father's guidance and did as his father had counseled. The young man ultimately was pleased with the decision, as he realized that if he had followed his instincts and desires, he would have left the job early, damaged the business, and fractured a vital relationship. This young man heeded his father's advice because the father had built a strong relationship with his son, who had learned to take advice and seek wisdom from his elders.

## "Love Covers a Multitude of Sins" (1 Peter 4:8)

Love will cover many sins, but it is essential to know what love looks like for a child and how an individual child receives and recognizes love (see Chapter 13 on Wisdom in Love and the love languages). Today's parents are time-poor, and it is easier to babysit with electronic devices, which are destructive to relationships, addictive, and may teach ideas damaging to children. With children, love means holding, physical touch, comforting, drying tears, and seeking to listen and understand what is in the child's heart. Simply, it means giving time to the child to understand who they are and to listen. We can find ourselves telling children many things but seldom find the time to hear them and understand their concerns. For a child, being listened to and affirmed in their individuality is one of the most important things. Parents need to put deposits into the child's "love bank" because these deposits of love and understanding will be there for the child to draw on when there are challenging times in the relationship with one or both parents.

# Intentional Time Together Over Meals, Reading the Word of God and Literature Classics

Some years ago, my family and I spent four months in a medium-sized French city where I was undertaking scientific research. We had many meals with French families and noted how different the mealtime tradition was from that in the U.S., U.K., or Australia. In these countries, for the most part, families seemed to eat as quickly as possible. One of the French hosts told me, "You English eat to live, but we live to eat." Notably, in France, each meal was a work of art, and the family sat around the table discussing politics, philosophy, and aspects of *"la condition humaine."* Time around the table is savored, and the meal and conversation are unhurried. Discussions range across all philosophical aspects of life from birth to death and what these ideas mean practically as we seek to live in the world. The evening meals often lasted for three to four hours. While there was occasional conflict due to differing views, we could see that relationships were strengthened through this intentional investment of time.

It is a life-giving practice to take time over a meal and hear from each family member. It also is invaluable to read something from God's ancient wisdom, the Bible, and explore it together. Reading aloud various literature classics together is also encouraging and strengthening to family life. However, it is essential to know that often there will be significant resistance to this idea from family members. It will likely be necessary to work through any opposition to the concept. Start with small steps to create meaningful family times over meals.

251

# Conclusions and Some Final Parenting Tips

Parenting is one of life's greatest joys and, at the same time, among the most challenging tasks we face. It is an assignment that is never finished. We must remember that it is often easier to inadvertently cause hurt and pain than to affirm, encourage, and love. Here are a few final tips to accompany the ancient wisdom from the Bible writers:

- Each child is an individual, and parents need to invest time to understand each child's disposition and heart, talents and interests, and strengths and weaknesses. It is essential to be interested in and support what each child cares about.

- As discussed in Chapter 6 (Wisdom in Communication), active listening with your children is essential. Take time so your child knows they have been heard, listened to, and understood rather than just talked at.

- Boundary setting and appropriate discipline are essential from the earliest days that the child can understand. Let your "'yes' be your 'yes,' and your 'no' your 'no.'"

- Your own behavior is the best teacher, so as a parent, you need to model the behavior you want to see. Children find copying what you do easier than listening to what you say.

- Encouraging independence is essential for children to grow into healthy adults who can take responsibility for their own lives. Of course, this needs to be age appropriate. When the child is older, particularly in the teenage years, it is essential not to interfere with the "law of sowing and reaping" by seeking to give a soft landing where bad decisions have been made. Instead, let the child learn through the experience of the consequences of their choices. This is a built-in teaching device designed by the Creator. To override it robs a child of the opportunity to learn and take responsibility for their decisions.

- The education system has become hijacked by an agenda that is at odds with God's law and values. Great care needs to be taken in deciding each child's education.

- In the case of siblings, it is vital to avoid comparing children. Such comparisons have done much harm over time and can lead to long-term sibling conflict.

# KEY POINTS ABOUT WISDOM IN PARENTING

- Parenting is more about teaching right relationships than simply teaching proper behavior.

- Although foreign to the modern mind, children must grow up with a "fear of the Lord," as this is the foundation for them to learn wisdom.

- The timeless, ancient wisdom of the Bible is vital to teach and emphasize in a world where everything is relative and changeable. Children need to be taught right relationships from the wisdom of the Bible to grow in understanding of the wise way to live.

- Children need to be taught respect and obedience to their parents. The Book of Proverbs says, "Whoever loves instruction loves knowledge, but he who hates correction is stupid" (Proverbs 12:1). *"Honor your father and your mother, that your days may be long in the land that the Lord your God is giving you"* (Exodus 20:12).

- Take time to listen and affirm your children.

- Love covers a multitude of sins, so love is the crucial ingredient to parenting. For each child, what love looks like will vary, and it is essential to understand how to love.

- Children need to learn that correction and discipline are carried out by parents because they love them, and children need to learn the "right way to go" for their own welfare (Proverbs 3:11–12).

- Children must be taught not to respond to discipline with resentment or sullenness. If this attitude is not corrected, it will become embedded in a child's character (Proverbs 12:1).

- Discipline must be given carefully and judiciously and never in anger. The punishment must always meet the crime (Colossians 3:21; Ephesians 6:4).

- Two fundamental and non-negotiable principles for parents are unity and consistency. Intentionally work on family boundaries and rules, and don't deviate from these. Let your "yes" be your "yes," and your "no" your "no."

- As a parent, invest time daily to know and understand each child's heart—what brings life and strength, their interests and passions, what they enjoy, and what leaves them feeling despondent.

- Intentional listening: take time so that your child knows that they have been heard, listened to, and understood, rather than just talked at. Be intentional about affirming your children. Learn what love looks like for each of your children. Love is the foundation of all family relationships.

- Setting aside time for the family to be together is essential. The evening meal is a wonderful opportunity to build and strengthen relationships, hear what is on the heart of your children, and engage in family conversations about life. It also is an excellent place to practice the art of storytelling.

In considering wisdom, we will conclude our journey in the following chapter by bringing many of the ideas we have explored together by considering the importance of the seasons of life.

# CHAPTER 16
# WISDOM IN UNDERSTANDING
# THE SEASONS OF LIFE

*"To everything, there is a season, A time for every purpose under heaven." (Ecclesiastes 3:1)*

One of the things that impacted me powerfully when I was part of a group of CEOs many years ago was the advice at the start of each year to reflect on your life from the viewpoint of your funeral and ask the question: how would you like to be remembered and what would you like those closest to say about you? This is not necessarily easy, but something that is worthwhile at any stage of life. Of course, as you age, there is more to reflect on and more mistakes to consider. I have done this review process for almost 25 years, and as I realize my many mistakes, I seem to be becoming more aware of the negative things people could say at my funeral. However, I also have learned that not all periods in life are the same, and it is crucial to understand the seasons of life you are in as you consider the opportunities and challenges ahead. Understanding these things will not only increase our peace but also determine where to set our focus at any time.

Although King Solomon wrote the Book of Ecclesiastes more than 3,000 years ago, I was deeply impacted by the wisdom in this book when I first heard the 1960s song by the Byrds, "Turn! Turn! Turn!"

The song's lyrics were accurate to the book, and in this chapter on wisdom, we will consider the significance of this part of Solomon's writings:

"To everything, there is a season,

A time for every purpose under heaven:

A time to be born,

And a time to die;

A time to plant,

And a time to pluck what is planted;

A time to kill,

And a time to heal;

A time to break down,

And a time to build up;

A time to weep,

And a time to laugh;

A time to mourn,

And a time to dance;

A time to cast away stones,

And a time to gather stones;

A time to embrace,

And a time to refrain from embracing;

A time to gain,

And a time to lose;

A time to keep,

And a time to throw away;

A time to tear,

And a time to sew;

A time to keep silence,

And a time to speak;

A time to love,

And a time to hate;

A time of war,

And a time of peace."

(Ecclesiastes 3:1–8)

The richness of wisdom in these verses is immense, and we will explore them in this chapter. Many people quote the above segment of Ecclesiastes, but it is interesting to note the verses that follow:

"He has made everything beautiful in its time. Also, He has put eternity in their hearts, except that no one can find out the work that God does from beginning to end.

I know that nothing is better for them than to rejoice, and to do good in their lives, and also that every man should eat and drink and enjoy the good of all his labor—it is the gift of God" (Ecclesiastes 3:11–13).

What an excellent set of verses to encourage us:

- God has formed the universe so that "everything is beautiful in its time." We will have seasons where the sun shines, and everything seems perfect and complete. However, we can put our trust in God, even when things look dire on every front, because He has said He will bring all things to their right place and alignment.

- God has put eternity in our hearts. We are physical beings, but we are also spiritual beings, bound for eternity. St. Augustine of Hippo, the fourth-century Christian philosopher, wrote: "You have made us for yourself, O Lord, and our heart is restless until it rests in You."[85] Across time, all civilizations have sought meaning and purpose beyond the physical and temporal.

- Finding out what God does "from beginning to end" is useless because we will never know. The point, however, is that God is trustworthy, and we can trust in Him and "lean not on our own understanding" (Proverbs 3:5). After all, God is God!

- Given what God has done for us, we need to rejoice or be joyful. Our response in thankfulness to God is to do good.

- We must enjoy the fruits of our labor and appreciate our food and drink because these are God-given gifts.

# The Biblical Seasons of Life

Reading through the Old Testament, it is clear that lifespans were much longer in ancient times. Before the Great Flood, many people lived to 800 or 900 years of age. What an opportunity to become wise with age! Job alluded to this when he said, "Wisdom is with aged men, And with length of days, understanding" (Job 12:12).

King Solomon wrote about the seasons of life, and undoubtedly, there was a linkage in his thoughts to the natural seasons. Each of the natural seasons has its own time frame, which then passes to the next season. Summer is a time of heat and dryness when storms can suddenly come, and drought can threaten. It is also the time for the ripening of crops. Autumn/fall is a time of change when the plants prepare themselves for dormancy through the cold ahead, and leaves fall. Winter is bleak and cold, and the days

---

85 https://www.crossroadsinitiative.com/media/articles/ourheartisrest-lessuntilitrestsinyou/

are short. Keeping warm is the most crucial focus. Spring renews hope as the first buds emerge, the ground warms, and plants come alive to set seed and produce abundance on the earth.

Understanding the alignment and connection of the seasons of our lives with the natural seasons is essential, particularly when we find ourselves in a difficult season. A problematic season will pass in the rhythm of seasons that come and go, and in God's grace, a new season of fruitfulness will open up. The advice of Winston Churchill is encouraging when we find ourselves in a difficult season: "When you are going through hell, keep going."[86]

Let's turn to the seasons identified by King Solomon and explore some of the relevance of these seasons in modern life. Though a book could be written on each of these critical seasons, here we will cover just a few key ideas.

## A Time to Be Born and a Time to Die (Ecclesiastes 3:2)

This first season is self-evident but essential. In his letter to the Ephesians, St. Paul tells us that "He chose us in Him before the foundation of the world" (Ephesians 1:4). We often think that life is a series of random events, but the Bible says that we were each chosen by God before the foundation of the world. King David said that God "formed my inward parts; You covered me in my mother's womb. I will praise You, for I am fearfully and wonderfully made" (Psalm 139:13–14).

We need to hold onto the truth of our lofty origins in and from God Himself and understand that every life, those born and unborn, is precious. Life is a gift from God; if we presume that we can make a

---

86  https://www.forbes.com/sites/geoffloftus/2012/05/09/if-youre-going-through-hell-keep-going-winston-churchill/?sh=54999773d549

decision to end a life, whether in the womb or in the mistaken idea that we can decide to end suffering, we are acting against God. He is the author, the giver and taker of life. King Solomon tells us that:

"The fear of the LORD prolongs days,

But the years of the wicked will be shortened" (Proverbs 10:27).

The Book of Job (Job 14:5) also states concerning humanity:

"Since his days are determined,

The number of his months is with You;

You have appointed his limits so that he cannot pass."

To interfere with God's sovereignty and wisdom in the bestowal and removal of life is to show no fear of the Lord and to invite judgment. Moses emphasized the truth of God's sovereignty and authority about life and the length of our lives. In his final speech to the children of Israel about to enter the Promised Lord, Moses explained blessing (if they chose God's way) and curse (if they turned away from God). Moses' admonition was:

"Therefore choose life … loving the LORD your God, obeying his voice and holding fast to him, for He is your life and length of days" (Deuteronomy 30:19–20).

As with all of God's truth, this is timeless wisdom: love and obey God because He is our life and determines the length of our days.

## A Time to Plant and a Time to Uproot What Has Been Planted (Ecclesiastes 3:2)

Farmers understand well the seasons of planting and reaping. There often is concern about whether the ground is ready for planting or those things which can interrupt the harvest. St. Paul gives further insight into God's fundamental law of the universe concerning what we plant and harvest: "Do not be deceived; God is not mocked; for whatever a man sows, he will also reap. For he who sows to his flesh will of the flesh reap corruption, but he who sows to the Spirit will of the Spirit reap everlasting life" (Galatians 6:7–8).

Robert Louis Stevenson expressed this idea most succinctly: "Sooner or later, everyone sits down to a banquet of consequences."[87] The consequences of what we have sown by our actions are helpful to us because if they cause us pain, we can learn from this and adjust what we do. In the seasons of life, the season of sowing (e.g., caring for others in a friendship, study, diligent work, etc.) may be extended before a season of reaping. We all need to learn to sow bountifully into people's lives and productive activities, and there may be reaping at an unexpected time.

## A Time to Kill and a Time to Heal (Ecclesiastes 3:3)

Is there a time to kill? This has been an age-old question for Christians, and many cite the Ten Commandments, notably Commandment Six—sometimes translated as "Thou shall not kill." However, the Hebrew word is רָצַח (transliterated as *râṣah*), which means murder (premeditated, unlawful taking of a life).[88] There are occasions when killing (the taking of a life)[87] is necessary, such as in self-defense and war. The penalty for proven murder in the Old Testament was death, which was used in most Western jurisdictions up until recent times. Killing, though, negatively impacts those who cannot avoid this, such as those in the army at war. The widespread problem of post-traumatic stress disorder (PTSD) in army veterans is a symptom of the impact that the violence of war

---

87  https://undefeatedmotivation.com/quotes/everybody-soon-or-late-sits-down-to-a-banquet-of-consequences-robert-ouis-stevenson-quote/

88  https://bibleask.org/what-is-the-difference-between-killing-and-murder/

and the trauma of killing often have on psychological well-being. If there is a season where killing is necessary, it should be recognized that the season for healing may be significantly prolonged as issues like PTSD are not easily treated.

Our bodies are designed to heal, but emotional wounds are far more challenging. The complexity of this is wonderfully covered in the important book by Dr. Bessel van der Kolk, *The Body Keeps the Score*.[89] We all deal with trauma in different ways, but many of these are inappropriate (e.g., drugs, alcohol, etc.) as we seek to escape from pain.

## A Time to Break Down and a Time to Build Up (Ecclesiastes 3:3)

Currently, videos are posted about coal-fired power stations being blown up to "protect the environment." It is easy to see that breaking something down is far easier than building something up. Nonetheless, there are seasons where breaking down is the best option: in the demolition of a building or bridge that is no longer safe, in the change of a government, in the redesign of curricula, and even, at times, in relationships. It is evident that in relationships that have been through painful events and seasons, trying to rebuild the relationship again quickly is not always wise. With our relationships, time is often needed for personal healing and waiting until the season is right for rebuilding.

## A Time to Weep and a Time to Laugh; A Time to Mourn and a Time to Dance (Ecclesiastes 3:4)

There is much to learn in the Book of Job, one of the most ancient wisdom texts. Job suffers an extraordinary and horrific range of

---

89  https://www.besselvanderkolk.com/resources/the-body-keeps-the-score

calamities in his life, with the loss of family, possessions, animals, and livelihood within a brief period. Job's wife provides the worst advice ever: "Curse God and die" (Job 2:9). Job's response shows extraordinary humility and faith as he tells his wife, "Shall we indeed accept good from God, and shall we not accept adversity" (Job 2:10). Job's wife failed to understand that as hard as it was to accept, they had entered a season for weeping. Job's friends who came to comfort him did profoundly understand this, and the narrative tells us that they were horrified when they saw Job and the state he was in. In response: "They sat down with him on the ground seven days and seven nights, and no one spoke a word to him, for they saw that his grief was very great" (Job 2:13).

Unfortunately, after first showing great empathy and understanding of Job's difficulties, his friends decided to berate him, and their thinking was simple: God rewards the good and punishes the wicked. We all know from personal experience that this is not true.

At some stage in our lives, we will find ourselves in a season of mourning. Seasons of laughter and joy will surely come but may not come for an extended period. If we have a friend in a season of mourning, we need to resist trying to diagnose the issue and giving advice because there are many unknowns—in the case of Job, Satan had been allowed to intervene and cause Job trouble for a season. It is crucial to stay on the side of simply caring and weeping with any person in a situation of great pain because this can be enough. In such cases, a person needs only to be heard and understood. It is essential that a season of mourning run its course, for a person must have time to process their loss. However, prolonged seasons of mourning may need intervention by someone with Godly wisdom as there may need to be an exploration of hidden areas of emotional pain that require healing.

## A Time to Cast Away Stones and a Time to Gather Stones; A Time to Keep and a Time to Throw Away (Ecclesiastes 3:5 and 3:6)

It is fascinating to see that Marie Kondo, the home and wardrobe organizational consultant, has become a celebrity and made a significant fortune out of straightforward advice about when to "cast away stones." Her focus is on decluttering and doing this by asking, for example, with an item of clothing, "Do you love it?" If you don't, she says, get rid of it.[90] We all seem capable of "gathering stones"; for some, it is difficult to "cast them away." Often you only realize how much you have gathered when it is time to move house, and you know you have many unnecessary items and may have spent too many seasons of "gathering stones." We all recognize that when it comes to the season of rationalizing and throwing away, we may have unnecessarily prolonged a season of gathering. When my mother was in her 80s, she had a season of giving away various precious items, and I saw what delight this gave her.

In King Solomon's time, the phrase may have been meant more literally and may have been related to gathering stones to cast onto enemies' fields.

However, for us, across the seasons of our lives and changing contexts, there are times we need to gather resources and also times we need to relinquish them.

## A Time to Embrace and a Time to Refrain From Embracing (Ecclesiastes 3:5)

The word translated as embrace is the Hebrew word חָבַק trans-literated as *ḥâḇaq*. It is often used to describe the embrace of a family member or someone of the same sex. For example, Laban

---

90  https://konmari.com/marie-kondo-rules-of-tidying-sparks-joy/

ran to embrace Jacob (Genesis 29:13) when he realized Jacob was his nephew, and Esau embraced his brother Jacob when he returned from exile (Genesis 33:4). The same word can also be translated as "folding of the hands" and is used in the Song of Songs to indicate romantic touch. Suppose you watch an English period film set in the 18th century. In that case, it is clear that the awareness in society at that time of the necessity of chaperoning young women to ensure that there was a "refrain from embracing" was paramount. This situation continued into the 20th century and even until today in some religious communities. We, in the West, seem to have forgotten that there is a season to refrain from embracing, particularly the opposite sex, and in developing romantic relationships. There would be much less pain, distress, and mental health issues if we took seriously the idea of a "time to refrain from embracing." There is a particular danger in romantic relationships in the workplace, as demonstrated almost daily in new stories about sexual harassment and office affairs that have ended badly.

## A Time to Gain and a Time to Lose; A Time to Tear and a Time to Sew (Ecclesiastes 3:6 and 3:7)

It is interesting to think that Solomon, who had greater riches than anyone before him or since wrote that there was a time to lose and gain. Gaining or acquiring something has its dangers, as material possessions can become something we love above all else. As discussed previously, Jesus was very clear about these dangers when He said:

"Do not lay up for yourselves treasures on earth, where moth and rust destroy and where thieves break in and steal; but lay up for yourselves treasures in heaven, where neither moth nor rust destroys and where thieves do not break in and steal. For where your treasure is, there your heart will be also" (Matthew 6:19–21).

However, there is a season for gain: to acquire land and a house or other possessions, save money for an essential purpose, or gain knowledge by studying.

Losing, on the other hand, is nearly always tricky for us. However, there may be a season for loss, and the most potent example I remember was a talk by Steve Jobs when he gave the commencement address to students at Stanford University in 2005.[91] Even though the video is now quite old, its messages are still compelling as he describes what happened after the Board of Apple dismissed him. This terrible event, the company founder being dismissed by the Board, resulted in remarkable productivity and innovation that otherwise would not have happened. If we experience similar loss in the form of failure, we too should consider not fighting against it but instead, consider what this apparent season of failure and loss may be teaching us. The verse about tearing and sewing is interesting because, in ancient times, people often tore their garments in the face of terrible loss or grief. Clearly, when we experience significant loss, we can feel that our lives are being torn apart. However, there is a time for sewing that involves restoration and rebuilding, which may be appropriate for damaged relationships or even property. Sometimes, it is simply setting our hearts to the process of putting the broken pieces of our lives back together.

## A Time to Keep Silence and a Time to Speak (Ecclesiastes 3:7)

My father had a good saying: "When in doubt, say nothing." One of life's greatest challenges is knowing when it is a time or season to

---

91  https://youtu.be/UF8uR6Z6KLc

be silent. In some of our cases, this may need to be a long season! It may be a season where we may simply need to be like Job's friends who sat with him in his grief and said nothing. There also are times when people around us, whether family, friends, or workmates, are not ready to hear something of importance to us. However, more often in our lives, silence is essential for us to listen and hear what is being said. All of us are more adept at speaking than listening, and we should cultivate the skill of being silent and listening. As discussed in an earlier chapter, when it is time to speak, rather than giving our opinions or advice, it may be better to consider asking questions (see Chapter 5 on Wisdom in Friendship). When emotions run high, asking questions is difficult to remember but can be a powerful opportunity to open up understanding.

## A Time to Love and a Time to Hate; A Time of War and a Time of Peace (Ecclesiastes 3:8)

Interestingly, Solomon ties love and hate together with peace and war. We know that God is love, and we have explored this more closely in a previous chapter. While often, to our human under-standing, "hate" is a poor response, the Book of Proverbs tells us that there are several things that God hates:

"These six things the LORD hates,

Yes, seven are an abomination to Him:

A proud look,

A lying tongue,

Hands that shed innocent blood,

A heart that devises wicked plans,

Feet that are swift in running to evil,

A false witness who speaks lies,

And one who sows discord among brethren" (Proverbs 6:16–19).

If God hates these things, then hate is a legitimate and proper response in some situations as defined by God. We should hate the things God hates, but our characters tend to be frail, so we end up hating people for what they have done rather than hating their behavior. On the other hand, God tells us that love covers a multitude of sins (Proverbs 10:12, 1 Peter 4:8). Our best response in most situations is love and forgiveness. Still, forgiveness does not necessarily mean reconciliation or ignoring what was done. It is right to seek justice for wrongdoing, even if it is wrong to cling to hatred in our hearts, because otherwise, as outlined in Chapter 7, we will be "handed over to the torturers" (Matthew 18:21–35).

It may be that the time for war is recognized too late. The season for war is more difficult for most of us to contemplate. Still, if we think back to World War II and the peace initiatives by the United Kingdom that kept failing, eventually, it became clear that war was the only solution to the predation of Nazi Germany. It is evident that in the 1930s in the United Kingdom and Europe, there was a denial of the significance of the re-arming of Germany, and when action was finally taken, it was almost too late. George Washington noted that "to be prepared for war is the most effective means of preserving peace."[92] King Arthur's speech in the film *First Knight* also is relevant when he says, "There is a peace only to be found on the other side of war."[93] Ultimately, this was the situation during World War II, and the failure to prepare for war almost resulted in the domination of the West by the Nazis.

In the big picture of our lives, the Bible tells us that the greatest war of all time lies ahead. Jesus has promised to return to reclaim

---

92  https://www.mountvernon.org/library/digitalhistory/past-projects/quotes/article/to-be-prepared-for-war-is-one-of-the-most-effectual-means-of-preserving-peace/

93  https://www.quotes.net/mquote/32463

the earth and drive off all evil. Only then will there be everlasting peace and the end of war. Then we will see the destruction of hate and the rule of love (Isaiah 9:6–7).

# KEY POINTS ABOUT WISDOM AND THE SEASONS OF LIFE

- God has put eternity in our hearts and made everything complete and beautiful in its time.

- It is essential to understand that life is made up of seasons and to understand the nature of these seasons.

- In life, we must consider the season we are in and determine what is appropriate for that season. This is especially true when we are in a difficult season. This difficult season will eventually pass.

- There is a time for every purpose under heaven: a time to be born, a time to die, a time to plant, a time to harvest, a time to kill, a time to heal, a time to tear down, a time to build, a time to mourn, a time to dance, a time for war, a time for peace, a time to be silent, and a time to speak.

- In the challenging seasons of life, it is essential to trust God and simply keep going, knowing there will be a new season of joy at some stage. As Winston Churchill said, "When you are going through hell, keep going!"[94]

---

94  https://www.forbes.com/sites/geoffloftus/2012/05/09/if-youre-going-through-hell-keep-going-winston-churchill/?sh=5394fc57d549

# CONCLUSIONS

In many ways, wisdom is an elusive idea and not commonly sought after in our post-modern world. One of the challenges of wisdom is that you may only know it when you see it. A simple definition of biblical wisdom is "the practical skills associated with living a successful life", and while this definition is helpful, it doesn't grasp the essence of wisdom as something that resides in and comes from God Himself. Also, we must understand what God means when He says "successful." Only a growing knowledge of God from the Bible will help us know what success is. St. Paul tells us that Jesus is the power of God, and He is the wisdom of God (1 Corinthians 1:24). Wisdom is a characteristic of God and comes from God. There is no wisdom outside of Him because He embedded into the tapestry of the universe. Wisdom is a characteristic that God has built into creation, waiting for us to discover and learn. This task is not easy in a world that has moved away from God. Wisdom often can be hidden from us because we have chosen our way to live rather than following God's ancient path and the timeless instruction and wisdom that He has provided for humans across the generations in the Bible.

To live happy, fulfilled, and successful lives, we need to be conscious of areas where we can be prone to make rash decisions. It is only in the seasons of our lives when we are in crisis, often due to our own bad choices, that the wisdom of ancient times comes to the fore. When we are impacted by the consequences of what we've done, we stop and review our lives. The Bible tells us that God has built an essential principle into the world, which is the "law of sowing and reaping" (Galatians 6:7). We can learn from our mistakes (when we sow badly and reap the consequences). If we can humble ourselves in the face of the consequences of our bad decisions and learn from them, we can make better decisions the next time we face similar circumstances. It is essential for those around us who love us not to interfere with this law because if we choose unwisely but receive a "soft landing" because a parent or friend intervenes, we don't suffer the consequences of our actions. So we don't learn and grow from the circumstances. For example, if we run up a credit card bill with unwise spending of money that we don't have, and our parents pay it off because they feel sorry for us, then we learn that we can spend without restraint, and someone else will take responsibility and fix the problem for us. So, we won't grow in wisdom or character.

We live at a time when society's traditional norms are increasingly being turned upside down in the name of "progress." Such is the challenge of modernity and post-modernism that there is now even the loss of the foundational belief in the existence of objective truth. Nonetheless, we live in a world where the consequences of our actions cannot be escaped. God revealed the law of sowing and reaping and learning the consequences of our efforts to ancient writers of the Bible. This law is still relevant today.

At the heart of wisdom is "the fear of the Lord," which is spoken about throughout the Old Testament and described as being "the beginning of wisdom" (Psalm 111:10, Proverbs 1:7, Proverbs 9:10, Job 28:28). The "fear of the Lord" is the foundation of wisdom. While the "fear of the Lord" has many dimensions, at its heart, it describes fundamental awe, reverence, and respect for the God of creation and a preparedness to accept His laws and precepts. The fear of the Lord does acknowledge that God is a God who hates wickedness (evil) and loves righteousness (blamelessness) and that He is a holy (set apart) God, who, while He loves us, needs to be approached with deep reverence and respect. Conversely, if we seek to define right and wrong outside of God's standards, we lack wisdom because we have no fear of the Lord. This is the path of foolishness and cannot lead to life.

Wisdom is based on an understanding and foundation that God's laws and His whole creation operate on principles designed to help us prosper if we grow in learning His ways and teaching these to others, especially our children if we are parents. The Bible contains God's ancient wisdom and imparts the ways of His wisdom that increasingly are essential in a world that has lost its way and seems to be affirming what is evil as good and what is good as evil, spoken about by the Old Testament prophet, Isaiah (Isaiah 5:20).

My journey into wisdom has been long and painful, as I have learned and, by God's grace, been changed through the law of sowing and reaping in my life. Over the last decades, I have gained an understanding of the bedrock of the Bible as God's word, and many things have fallen into place. I have progressively understood God's Word and sought to apply it to my own life.

In this book, I have written about first-hand experiences related to vital areas where ancient biblical wisdom has informed and helped me re-orient my life around the instruction and wisdom of God in the Bible. The areas I have covered in the book chapters are hopefully comprehensive but are not designed to be exhaustive.

I have written about areas where God's ancient wisdom has impacted my life. I hope these observations will be helpful in the lives of others. I believe that God's ancient wisdom has impacted my life for good. Placing ancient wisdom before modern thinking will bring lasting contentment, confidence, and peace.

Though the Bible is among the most ancient writings, it is extraordinary and timeless and still is the bestselling book of all time. I read it daily, and it reveals new insights and wisdom each day. It is not just an ancient text containing incredible accounts of God's faithful interactions with people but a book that seeks to take us into the heart and mind of God Himself. For the last few years, I have felt an increasing sense of urgency to write this book because I have observed that the world has turned its back on God. God's ancient and ageless wisdom needs to be rediscovered and followed if there is hope for future generations.

I trust that in providing some insights and understanding of the relevance and application of the ancient ways of God to our modern world, this book might encourage you to pursue God and His wisdom. I believe both older and younger generations will be stirred to find the ancient wisdom that comes from God alone and walk in it (Proverbs 2:1–9). The solution for most of the ills of society can be found stated simply in the last book of the Old Testament, where God brings a message to His people through the prophet Malachi declaring: "... return to Me, and I will return to you ..." (Malachi 3:7). For each of us, God is calling us and asking us to humble ourselves and return to Him and His ways.

# ACKNOWLEDGMENTS

My wife Kate provided great and dedicated editing after I had completed the rough draft of the book. When I gave her my draft, I thought no further changes were needed. However, I was wrong, and Kate helped with better wording and significant edits that ensured the continuity and flow of the ideas. I am grateful for her insightful work and her love and dedication. I also am exceedingly thankful for her contribution to the book. I am also grateful for the excellent editing work of Sky Nuttall, who has greatly helped in preparing the book for publication, and Corey Stark from Ignite the Nations, for making editing suggestions and writing a foreword.

www.ingramcontent.com/pod-product-compliance
Lightning Source LLC
Chambersburg PA
CBHW060904120626
46553CB00001B/205

* 9 7 9 8 8 9 1 0 9 1 1 4 6 *